UNWAVERING
Love

JENNIFER C. WILLIAMS

Published by hope*books
2217 Matthews Township Pkwy
Suite D302
Matthews, NC 28105
www.hopebooks.com

hope*books is a division of hope*media

Printed in the United States of America

First paperback edition.
Paperback ISBN: 979-8-89185-213-6
Hardcover ISBN: 979-8-89185-159-7
Ebook ISBN: 979-8-89185-160-3
Library of Congress Number: 2025930645

hope*books
hopebooks.com

*Because the world needs your hope-filled
words now more than ever*

"When you've been betrayed by the most intimate relationship in your life, you need help to navigate crushing grief without becoming stuck in its grasp. You need a friend who has felt the death blow of divorce and managed to find life again. Jennifer Williams is that friend. 'Unwavering Love' is her gift to you, an embrace that holds you in the darkness and guides you to hope on the other side. She desires to companion you with grace-filled wisdom from the Bible, her journals, and sound spiritual teaching. Find your way to Jesus and allow love to mend your broken heart."

MINDY KIKER, Flourish Writers Co-Founder

"Jennifer doesn't shy away from sharing her own raw emotions that accompanied divorce. While acknowledging these emotions, she provides practical steps forward to healing and a new life securely centered within the love of our Heavenly Father. Her book is encouraging and reminds readers that God does not leave us alone in our time of need, whether that be a divorce or other life trials. Jennifer's poetic and deeply observant style of writing is in itself a gift to the reader, a lovely multifaceted gem for the soul to delight in."

BONNIE KNUDSEN

"Jennifer's book has helped me connect so many dots in my own world. Reading her words is a comfort and a compass. Jennifer is honest as she writes, and she continually brings us back to the space where we are safe to express our loss and grief, and while compassionately being led back into alignment with what God says, and who He is for us, in our most troubling moments.

We are not alone in our difficult season - in our pain and unraveling the Father is knitting us back together piece by piece. Jennifer shares her life and experience, and we are invited to join in our own context, to find peace and healing. I encourage you to read her book, and discover God's Unwavering Love for you!"

JENNIFER BRYANT-CHOONG,
Author of *Signs From God:*
Discovering God's Messages in Your Everyday Life
for Healing, Direction and Transformation

"In words straight from her heart, Jennifer Williams in this insightful piece of writing, well-suited for the Christmas season, charms and beckons to all of us needing comfort for times of grief and agony of the soul,

This book describes the challenges that the author faced in going through an unexpected divorce.

In many ways this is a practical "how-to" book describing how anyone facing a severe grief-causing event can find God's strength and faith to survive, and to ultimately gain the victory over the initial insult.

Stating "when grief arrives let it cause you to connect with God through prayer", she then describes having tea or coffee and welcoming conversation through prayer: "God is right there," she says. Jennifer clearly sensed God's presence; to her, Immanuel's Name truly means "God-with-us".

In her grief and sadness she learned "my sadness is much too heavy to lean on anything but Jesus." And further, "Jesus offers faith when we are full of fear...."

She reminisces and encourages in a summary of every lesson she has ever learned, saying "it seemed always to bring me back to the knowledge that I was created in the image of God."

Quite significantly, she discovered that in the practice of journaling and simply slowing down and studying the details of everyday life, a tremendous benefit resulted in facing her grief ! In essence she found that journaling was one of the most essential practices that she could do to combat grief!"

DOUG CASKEY

Table of Contents

Introduction

"Fret not yourself because of evildoers;
be not envious of wrongdoers!

For they will soon fade like the grass
and wither like the green herb.

Trust in the LORD, and do good;
dwell in the land and befriend faithfulness.

Delight yourself in the LORD,
and he will give you the desires of your heart."

Psalm 37:1-4

This book is about love: God's love and the frailty of human love. Through a divorce, I recognized how wrong I had been about my desires. When I thought I was doing something good, something from a place of love, by giving up my own desires for someone else, God showed me that my desires were small, intricate pieces of vitality placed there by Him, my Creator.

A desire is a gift from God because He loves me. It is not a hindrance to a holy life at all but an actual gift given because I delight in Him. Trusting that a desire may be from God turns out to draw me nearer to God, not further away, as I was led to believe. When aligned with God, the desires of the heart are like a compass given to us to guide us, not necessarily to happiness but to something much more deep and real: joy.

My marriage ended for many reasons, but I take responsibility for only my part: I did not recognize my belovedness and trust in that love above the earthly love of marriage. There were many things I thought were insignificant and didn't really matter, but in reality, I see how much they did matter. The blessing of being outside a marriage and looking in brings about a bittersweet clarity like this. Often, we don't even realize how a person or experience leaves a mark on us.

I see these markings, impressions, and patterns that are beginning to come together. They clue me in on the desires of my God-seeking heart. I don't know why we marry, and then we so often put this relationship on a pedestal, even to the detriment of our own soul and body. I don't believe human love is supposed to be like this.

I am still learning how to know God better, and in the process of understanding the depths of all that God, I'm gaining knowledge of myself. I am starting to see how truly my self-image touches every corner of my life. My confidence is in my Creator, who created me in his image. If I do not see myself as God sees me, my ability to love others is hindered. A spiritually healthy self-love enables me to love others better and God above anyone.

I know these themes about loving ourselves and understanding ourselves can make some uncomfortable. If you fear these things as wrong or selfish, point yourself back to Jesus' greatest commandments:

"Teacher, which is the great commandment in the Law?" And he said to him, 'You shall love the Lord your God with all your heart and with all your soul and with all your mind. This is the great and first commandment. And a second is like it: You shall love your neighbor as yourself.'"

Matthew 22:36-39

God knows when we search with every inch of our being. We search for Him, and we also search for ourselves. We search for love and connection. We find all of these things eventually. But the word search invokes an image of digging deeply or climbing high up on shelves or rooftops. To search is so much more than a glance around.

God has met me amid every tearful episode. He has rescued me from dangerous thoughts that would only lead to inflicting this grief upon someone else I love. The tears, thoughts of suicide, and fears that have paralyzed me. I've noticed how they are still here, but the power they have over me gets weaker every time I speak an honest prayer to my God.

This book is my experience of going through divorce and the grief that still, at times, makes me unsteady. Every devotional has a note from the journals I kept during my first two years of being separated and divorced. I share my thoughts on God's faithful love and the words that helped me the most. I hope what has helped me take one small next step will also give you assurance that you still are not alone or forsaken. Every lesson learned seemed to bring me back to the knowledge that I was created in the image of God.

I forgot, not just once but many times along the way, who I was in relation to God. I was still the same young girl who had prayed to Jesus to fill my heart one night as I sat on a windowsill gazing up at a beautiful full moon. I prayed. I felt his presence immediately, and that was enough for me to believe in Him and say yes to his invitation to love me forever.

I am learning how to watch expectantly because I know He answers me with what is good for my senses and best for my soul. This is hard when I disagree about what is best. I've noticed when I let go and leave it in His hands everything seems to turn out better than I ever imagined. God has such a beautiful way of changing my mind and my heart or emotions. I put down my ideas and agendas of how things need to work out. It is in this I think I delight the most in God.

I still have days of falling and betraying myself as well as my God, but I don't dwell there.

I have discovered a home within my soul, and I believe it is an unshakeable one. Nothing but my own uncaptured thoughts can shake this home loose. I dwell here and feed upon his faithfulness.

My food to eat is the truly nourishing. The deepest cold water is brought up from the center of darkness. God is a master at feeding his beloved and quenching their thirst. Our souls are always nourished and skillfully worked upon by Him. Through my grief, I felt many times like I was being set aside physically by the man I loved and spiritually by the God who loved me, yet I learned how very different both their agendas were.

In listening and responding to a man's love that failed me and God's love that held me tighter than I ever imagined possible, I was beginning to see that I had been putting too much of my trust in the idol of marriage. I had always sensed that marriage was not a bad thing, but my abandonment of myself for marriage was not good. It was giving up more than God desired for me to give up.

Marriage isn't an end to our identity. We are still God's beloved, first and foremost. I believe this to be true: God can take us out of an unhealthy marriage. I am learning that God is the author of my circumstances, and I get to either exert my will toward beauty, life, and goodness versus ugliness, death, and the merely acceptable.

I desire to trust and obey because this seems to be why and how to find Christ in the bright afternoon light like a woman did at the well. I need to walk unapologetically into the open air and sunlight. God enfleshed asks me, as a woman divorced and feeling broken, for a drink of water. I am deep in all the other wrong ways of being. Yet I am asked by Jesus Christ for something I doubt I should give because who am I?

> "A woman from Samaria came to draw water. Jesus said to her, "Give me a drink."
>
> The Samaritan woman said to him, "How is it that you, a Jew, ask for a drink from me, a woman of Samaria?"... Jesus answered her, "If you knew the gift of God, and who it is that is saying to you, 'Give me a drink,' you would have asked him, and he would have given you living water." The woman said to him, "Sir, you have nothing to draw water with, and the well is deep..."
>
> John 4:7, 9-11

Jesus already knows exactly who I am. He asks questions that are more for our benefit than His. I sometimes do not recognize Jesus. The woman at the well didn't recognize Jesus. I am the one who asks, "How can you possibly take care of me?" Just like the woman said, "Sir, you have nothing to draw water with." So how?

How does Jesus provide the nourishment I want and need when it looks like there are no tools to do the job? There is no bucket to draw water, and the well is deep. It appeared Jesus was offering something impossible to attain. My spiritual eyes needed to open up because my physical eyes saw only a wrecked life with no way to go on.

This book is some of the hows. A chronicling of my own soul experiencing Jesus doing impossible and socially surprising things. This book is divided into days with helpful hints and journal snippets. These are words I hope will encourage you to turn to the God who pursues us lovingly and faithfully, never leaving us behind. I hope you grieve fully and begin to heal and take a step into life again whenever you are ready.

Remembrance

"The LORD is near to the brokenhearted and
saves the crushed in spirit."

Psalm 34:18

A Note From My Journal: If I don't want to choose death, then I have to figure out how to live. How to keep breathing. It's all so sad.

It was Christmas Day, and I knew my marriage of 30 years was over. I could tell you all the details right here and now, but that seems futile because you are probably reading this from your own painful circumstances. So let's just agree to hold each other's pain gently and carefully without judgment, and we will see what details come up naturally.

I welcome you to this space of ink and paper and the thoughts that leaked out of me during some of the worst days of my life. I hope it helps to know you're not alone. Divorce isn't ever simple and easygoing for anyone who honors truth and loves fully. It's not easy to move along in some sort of "conscious uncoupling" way. I was truly devastated at the loss of my married life.

Divorce for me felt like thirty years of my life were used up. My love was wasted. My body denied the years I needed someone the most. My work unconsidered.

All that I thought was precious was cast aside, like pearls thrown into the mud with swine to trample. Divorce is a death with an epitaph that proclaims, "I'm dead, and I no longer love you." It was mourning someone still alive who had promised to love me and cherish me. He was able to love me but chose not to do so.

It's the moments before grief settles in or rage is released that look and feel the most like denial. This is right before the crushing and breaking.

It's like holding glass and tripping on the unexpected. The glass is falling, but maybe I can reach out and catch it before it lands on the hardwood floor. Of course, I can't. It's all too unexpected, and I'm thrown off balance.

My heart is breaking as the man I love tells me he no longer loves me. He tells me difficult but true things. Finally, truthful things that free me from loving him. However, being freed can feel like being homeless. I had somehow wrapped my entire identity into being this man's wife.

I identified as the love of his life. I felt certainty in our mutual plans going in one direction. I thought he was mine. I thought I was his.

How meaningless and wasted my life felt in that moment of being told he had tried to stay in love, but he just couldn't do it anymore. How light my promises seemed to him. How unimportant I must have been for a very long time. I felt some sort of crushing deep within my spirit.

I couldn't stop crying, and I needed to understand why this was happening. I wanted to blame someone, but who? Late one night I felt audacious enough to wonder for a moment about God and about how I thought I'd done all the right things.

Where was I going to place my heart? I was in a bedroom of our house alone, maybe it was midnight, I'm not sure, but I knew at that moment my Father in heaven could not be blamed. Do you ever feel like God has just proved Himself to be so real, so true, so all-present too many times for your soul to doubt Him or blame Him?

I knew I would never make it if I thought my God was cruel. I had to remember who He had always been. How slowly God had walked with me through all my doubts about Him in my twenties and some of my thirties. There were years when I thought I could not love a God who thought the way a certain religion did about women.

My Creator showed me the foolishness of men and women alike who thought they could confine sacred, beautiful souls. God placed books and examples of real people right in front of me. He rescued me from the lies that questioned my own mind's ability to understand his deep love. My God is the one who asked me questions like why I believe what I believe. He revealed the truth to me in the past so I would not have to live imprisoned by lies.

In the face of harsh circumstances, will I remember who my God is? Will bitterness take root, or will I trust all that I know Him to be? It takes mere seconds to sow a seed of bitterness or sow a seed of sweetness.

I cannot be bitter toward God. That breaks me completely and crushes the only faithful and unconditional love I've ever experienced. I pull my Bible out and turn the lamp on, and I read over and over again, "The Lord is near the broken-hearted and saves the crushed in spirit" Psalm 34:18.

A Step Towards Life:

Can you remember a time when God proved Himself faithful to you? Can you remember a time when you proved yourself faithful and trusting to him? Sometimes, we just need to be still and quiet, and a memory will come up.

Grief Arrives

"The people who survived the sword found grace in the wilderness; when Israel sought for rest, the LORD appeared to him from far away.

I have loved you with an everlasting love; therefore I have continued my faithfulness to you."

Jeremiah 31:2-3

A Note From My Journal: It is New Year's Eve. I sit outside on a dock, looking into a frozen lake. I am angry, and I don't know what to do with this emotion.

It is pointless to lie about the darkness that begs me to end my life. I can no longer pretend that grief has not arrived at my doorstep with bags and trunks full. Grief really must come inside, invited or not. She favors the weeping. She will rub your back and make you tea.

Divorce feels unreal, as if it isn't happening at all. But grief smiles and winks her eye, telling you it's shock. It is all real. Divorce is happening.

Divorce has landed us on the other side of love. Depending on our circumstances, this can look vastly different to each of us going through divorce. What hurts each of us most varies on what was valued most and what was cut out of our hopes and dreams for our marriage. We all have a different vision in mind when we walk down the aisle on our wedding day.

On the other side of love, it can feel so wobbly because actions have spoken loud and clear, but our hearts have not had the time to catch up. We need to find our balance and catch our breath because divorce casts us in our own unrecognizable wilderness. It is a shock to find yourself mentally and physically in an unfamiliar place.

I remember it being impossible to think of anything other than the fact that my husband wanted a divorce. Shock and anger pervaded every waking moment. I questioned everything. I wanted to hurt or at least blame someone.

These weren't feelings I was used to having on a daily basis. I knew from experience that to internalize this rage would only bring a familiar darkness to my soul. I didn't want to go backward. I had worked hard at my own tendencies towards depression.

I had overcome a lot, yet on this New Year's Eve, I wanted to die. I had no hope. I feared that feeling, that actual way of being where I would long to join in the happiness and life around me, but something inside me made it forbidden. A darkness that seemed to say, "Don't you dare."

I was no longer so young and naive. One of the first verses God opened up for me to see was Jeremiah 31:2-3. That last part of verse three, "I have loved you with an everlasting love therefore I have continued my faithfulness to you."

I might not have felt God's faithfulness or everlasting love in that moment, but I did know I had experienced it before, and if I experienced it before, surely I could experience it again.

God doesn't get angry when we tell Him how we feel or what we think. God knows already. Honestly talking to God about the depths of despair or anger you feel will not shock Him. Honesty will only release you to feel, cry, confront, say the things you need to say, and do the things you need to do.

Confessing our truth isn't for God's benefit. It is for our benefit, and that's why our loving God guides us to ask Him, seek Him, and find Him in the first place. Remember, God loved you first, not the other way around. We are invited and welcomed to prayer. He is delighted when we are in constant conversation with Him. We can find grace in the wilderness. When we think we are beyond God's reach, He meets us right there with his everlasting love. Prayer can be the main thing that gives us balance.

Communication and connection with God and with ourselves, as well as others who support and love us, can give us a direction to take a step towards. Where do you turn when you are evicted from all you thought was safe and a true home? You might feel alone, but God is right there.

As independent as we desire to act, at our core, we deeply want and need connection, love, and acceptance. When grief shows up, the worst thing we can do is ignore it. Grief is something to connect with, not run away from. We still have a need for connection, even if we try to tell ourselves we can make it on our own.

There is truth to this independence. We probably can make it. But what does that look like to you? Do you see a life lived abundantly or one lived in scarcity?

We each get to decide to set our own will towards life or towards death. We don't have to have every step figured out. Facing what is happening and what has already happened is emotionally painful and mentally exhausting. But it is worth it to deal with it here and now rather than burying it down only to erupt at some other time.

Believe it or not, you will survive. I know it doesn't seem like it, but you will, just like I did, just like many men and women have survived. Recognize your trauma, your anger, and your grief; don't let it slink away unobserved.

A Step Towards Life:

When grief arrives, let it cause you to connect with God through prayer. Have you ever just sat quietly in silence, having tea or coffee? Like a ritual, I call it the art of tea because it's calming and meditative, from putting water into a kettle to pouring it into your favorite mug. It's setting up an atmosphere in a small, uncomplicated way that welcomes conversation through your prayers or your silence and even your tears. God is right there.

Grief Observed

"...Behold, the dwelling place of God is with man. He will dwell with them, and they will be his people, and God himself will be with them as their God. He will wipe away every tear from their eyes, and death shall be no more, neither shall there be mourning, nor crying, nor pain anymore, for the former things have passed away."

Revelation 21:3-4

A Note From My Journal: Day 2 of the rest of my life. I read this from C.S. Lewis, he wrote it while going through grief after his wife Joy died. I find this speaks clearly for my soul: "For in grief nothing "stays put." One keeps on emerging from a phase, but it always recurs. Round and round. Everything repeats. Am I going in circles, or dare I hope I am on a spiral?

But if a spiral, am I going up or down it?

"How often -- will it be for always? -- how often will the vast emptiness astonish me like a complete novelty and make me say, 'I never realized my loss till this moment'? The same leg is cut off time after time."[1]

C.S. Lewis, A Grief Observed

There are common themes within grief, but each of us is unique in how or when we experience these themes. My experience was one of constant entering or leaving behind one emotion after another. One moment, I was denying that my husband no longer loved me,

---

1 Clerk, N. W. (pseud. of C. S. Lewis). *A Grief Observed*. Faber and Faber, 1961.

and the next I felt angry at my husband and at myself for still being in love. The imbalance of shifting from one emotion to the next can have us doubting we will ever make it through this grief.

There isn't necessarily any rhyme or reason to the stages of grief. Elizabeth Kubler-Ross explores the five stages of grief in her book, *On Death And Dying:*[2]

Denial

Anger

Bargaining

Depression

Acceptance

Your visit with grief is yours alone. Don't compare yourself to anyone else or let others make you feel bad because you aren't "over it" in the timeframe they think is appropriate. You might never be exactly the same, and there is nothing wrong with that. Try for progress over perfection each day.

Acknowledging and naming our feelings sets clarity in motion. Emotions aren't a bad thing. Emotions are indicators that something is not right and needs to be addressed, not ignored. When we are able to articulate how we feel, we not only understand ourselves better, but others will be able to hear and understand us better.

Grief begs to be addressed, acknowledged, and allowed to exist for a time. There is no shame in tears. There is no shame in feeling despair so strongly you regret you are even alive. Seek help from a mental healthcare professional. This does not take away from what God does to help us; rather, it only aids Him.

---

2 Kübler-Ross, Elizabeth. *On Death and Dying.* Simon & Schuster/Touchstone, 1969.

Walk into the wilderness with this companion named Grief. The strange thing is God greets you both there.

Like Elijah felt beneath the broom tree, "..It is enough; now, O Lord, take away my life, for I am no better than my fathers" (1 Kings 19:4). The beautiful part of this story is God fed Elijah and gave him water to drink. Elijah slept and woke up again and again to food and water. God knew that Elijah despaired of life. Elijah had already said to God, It is enough, O Lord, take away my life.

God is not shocked at our fear or our sadness. We can say we are done and cry tears of despair. What will God do? He lifts the burden from our shoulders. He becomes that strength that humbly moves us forward; it looks like gracefulness and restfulness.

He still loves me. He still loves you. Does He seem far away? God's love is everlasting, and his plan is to dwell within us and walk with us even as our emotions spiral in different directions.

We have an enemy that desires to only cause us more harm. He longs to steal our every accomplishment, convince us our love is meaningless, and destroy the beauty entangled with every beautiful memory.

A Step Towards Life:

You are alive. Take a deep breath.

In her book *Breath As Prayer*, Author Jennifer Tucker shares her experience of being in the hospital with her daughter. Feeling fearful and alone and at a loss for words to pray, she remembered reading about breath prayers. The words of one of the prayers came to her; they were a few lines from Psalm 23.

"I took a deep breath, and as I inhaled, I tried to focus my mind on the words, 'The Lord is my Shepherd,' and as I exhaled, I whispered, 'I have all that I need.'... As I focused on my breathing and the words of Scripture, my body calmed and my soul was reminded of a truth that will never change, no matter my circumstances."[3]

3   Tucker, Jennifer. *Breath as Prayer: Calm Your Anxiety, Focus Your Mind, and Renew Your Soul.* Thomas Nelson, 2022.

When We Need Help

"I lift up my eyes to the hills.
From where does my help come?

My help comes from the LORD,
who made heaven and earth.

He will not let your foot be moved;
he who keeps you will not slumber."

Psalm 121:1-3

A Note From My Journal: I had the wrong day. I drove all the way there… and then had a crying episode. A breakdown because I couldn't remember the day. I need to shut down for a little while.

———

This is the problem: I cannot trust where I cannot see. I see no future. I can't even imagine it, which is sort of terrifying for me.

My mind has always blessed me in the past with a creative vision of sorts. I could see glimpses of possibilities. I could plan it out step by step on my calendar.

But not now. Not with this. I wasn't going to be ok. I knew this deeply the day I went to a doctor's appointment on the wrong day. It wasn't the forgetfulness; it was my emotional reaction.

It was time to press pause on my life. Are you allowed to do that? I don't think it's a privilege for only a few.

"My God does not sleep or slumber.."

I am not so important that God needs me to ignore my grief. Nor does any work or children or anyone at all need me in this state of sadness. God cares much more about our relationship and the state of my soul than anything I could ever do. The world forgets and moves on with or without us, which might seem sad. But if you think about that, it may help us prioritize what goes into and out of our lives.

Ask yourself if you are going to be okay. I knew my answer to this was a no. I wasn't going to be fine. So many times in the past, I had convinced myself that I would be fine, I would be strong and get through whatever obstacle was in front of me, but this time was so different.

I was scared and sought professional help. I talked to a therapist on a regular basis until I felt strong enough to think honest and clear thoughts instead of harmful and jaded thoughts. This was what I needed to do. Maybe you need the same, or maybe not. Either way, extend yourself the courtesy of asking yourself what you really need. Doing this is a strength, not a weak or selfish endeavor.

This knowledge is between you and your Creator. Don't let anyone else have access to your mental, spiritual, or physical well-being. Pray for strength, and He will answer you. It takes thirty seconds to call someone for help. There will be some helpful phone numbers and websites in the appendix of this book.

This is not the time for a do-it-yourself therapy session. Despair, depression, violent angry feelings, and suicidal thoughts all indicate something is terribly wrong. There is nothing wrong with you for having these emotions. It is normal, but most of us need help getting things back into perspective.

If you are experiencing thoughts of suicide or a deep sense of hopelessness and you need immediate help, please call the National Suicide Hotline by dialing 988.

You can find locally trained therapists or church counselors. There are also online mental health care options that can give advice and prescribe medication. Life coaches specialize in certain areas like grief or divorce or transitioning into a new life. There are a lot of helpful options available for specific problems, so please reach out and take care of yourself.

It can feel good to talk to someone who isn't necessarily a friend or family member. It's advice from a neutral person, and it is kept confidential in a private setting. Here are some indicators that you may need help from a mental health professional, counselor, or coach:

1. Any plan to end your suffering by death or thoughts that say everyone would be better without you.
2. A dependency on alcohol or dangerous misuse of prescription drugs or illegal drugs.
3. Feelings of hopelessness and helplessness.
4. After a few months to a year, you are finding it hard to return to old or new responsibilities, routines, or things you enjoy.
5. Obsessive thoughts, doubting your self-worth, feeling paralyzed with dread and fear.
6. Extreme anger.
7. If you are not noticeably going through the stages of grief but seem stuck and neutral.
8. Either extreme of filling up every waking moment with activities or staying home and completely isolating yourself.

There is a lot of good help out there; the hardest part is getting started. It can feel strange to begin, but it is worth it in the long run. I always prayed before going to the therapist or the doctor. I prayed for the right words and right questions from the right person to get my mind and heart back to a place of alignment. You may still feel sad and falter often, but seeking help for mental health or physical health is a step towards healing.

You may need to cry or sleep for hours while someone else takes care of your responsibilities. Remember, it's just a pause. We can walk through grief much more gracefully, acknowledging it rather than ignoring it.

A Step Towards Life:

Take an honest evaluation of whether or not you might need some help. Whether it's from a trained professional or friends and family, we come out better when we take the time to acknowledge our needs and ask the appropriate person that can actually help.

You Are an Eternal Soul

"...You are wrong, because you know neither the Scriptures nor the power of God. For in the resurrection they neither marry nor are given in marriage, but are like angels in heaven. And as for the resurrection of the dead, have you not read what was said to you by God: 'I am the God of Abraham, and the God of Isaac, and the God of Jacob'? He is not God of the dead, but of the living."

Matthew 22:29-32

A Note From My Journal: I find it beautiful that Jesus says marriage isn't part of the kingdom of heaven. These brothers ask Jesus who the woman will belong to in heaven. And Jesus answers this way. As if to say she will belong to God alone. I don't have to be with a man here on earth nor through eternity My soul is mine and I give it trustingly back to my Creator.

The truth is a beloved daughter of God can be told she is no longer loved or wanted by the man who promised to love her. Marriage between two Christians who know and understand how God desires them to love each other can still fail miserably. Just because we have the knowledge doesn't mean we can implement that knowledge into our lives. Only God loves unconditionally and perfectly.

It seems the world takes marriage either much too lightly or much too seriously. Either way is some sort of perversion of what could be a beautiful gift from God. Marriage is a covenant, a holy promise that is supposed to mirror God's love for his people. Marriage is just one example of love. It doesn't mean that if you aren't married you aren't loved by God or you are of any less value as a single person. Putting the marriage upon a pedestal to worship sort of misses the point, but so does acting as if getting married is meaningless or getting divorced is just a natural part of life.

I felt invincible when it came to our marriage. It began so perfectly. I thought we had shared dreams. But the truth is I was very much on my own pretty soon after the marriage ceremony. I just don't think I understood at the time how serious it was to give up so many of my own dreams and goals so he could pursue so many of his own.

Even though I know we are warned that in this fallen world, we will experience suffering and heartbreak, it still catches you by surprise when it happens. I thought I would have more control of the way in which I suffered. When I did the right things, or at least what I thought were the right things, and I still suffered. I couldn't help but feel some anger.

God removed me from a marriage that was damaging me, and my ex-husband could probably say was damaging for him. It was a marriage that ended very badly. The comforting thing is knowing our worth, and our belovedness is not dependent on being married. It still hurts to go through a divorce and all the unexpectedness of life, love, and dreams dying.

Being newly single can have some difficult moments, but it can also be a time of renewal and transformation. It could be a time to consider your course in life and embrace the freedom you have to change and do new things without anyone else looking in.

Divorce has brought me some peace and a new joy in learning what I desire instead of settling for less than what I want to appease someone else. Divorce can be an initiation into a greater sense of wholeness. This could be a time of healing old wounds and putting all the fragments of life together like a puzzle. A time to catch up on what God has been whispering within your heart about who you are and who He desires to be to your soul.

A Step Towards Life:

You no longer have the title of wife. A new season has come. Ask yourself, "Who am I?" and "What kind of a woman do I want to be now?" There are old ways of being that no one can take away from you, along with ways of being that do not fit you at all anymore. You are still a beloved child of God. He is so good at turning the things that are meant to harm us into beautiful, healing things that bring us newness of life.

Be curious about the good and the bad of this new season of life that may strip you of one identity but give you a brand new identity. This could be a chance to reinvent yourself.

This could be a beautiful time of renewal and transformation as you embrace new things. Tune into the whispers of your own soul. Remind yourself of what you have already accomplished this far in life. Dream new ways, write them down, and decide what you really want and need.

God's Gift of Nature

"He gives snow like wool;

he scatters frost like ashes.

He hurls down his crystals of ice like crumbs;

who can stand before his cold?"

Psalm 147:16-17

A Note From My Journal: It snows outside my window. I know the birds are still fed. Do they ever even ask? When I cannot focus, and I have hardly any words, it is then that your words rescue me.

Swift words float through my mind. I cannot keep them. I cannot hoard them. Your words are for right now because that is the power of the living and breathing words of God.

———

I woke up to snow this morning—the first snow in my new home. It captivated me the same way it did when I lived in the woods with the man I loved. The pristine white layer of snow that my childish soul claims as her own meant to be.

My normal schedule is cast aside on this snow day. I drink hot black coffee slowly first thing and put on leggings and warm socks. I layer a T-shirt, sweater, jacket, and a hat. I begin walking my mile and say to myself, "I don't need to time it today."

I think about a life lived with the things I want or need to do noted in ink and paper but not set to the confines of time. What if I let rhythms come and go based on a measured level of how much

I am still enjoying any given activity? The storms will always keep coming like the snow came today. I say, "Let them." I'm bundled up warm, and my soul feels happy right now.

It's easy to say "let them" right now. But still, I'm in the midst of unhappiness, hurt, and grief. The bigger picture is that life is here and now, not in the future nor in the past. We are tried, tested, and tempest-tossed.

For some, the cold has a scent. A clean, clear scent with a rushing freshness that threatens my lungs to keep breathing or die. A scent that feels like sharp points of quickly freezing breath. I can see my own breath as I walk.

I am reminded that the breath of God is given to each of us. He gives snow gently and scatters the frost all over. I am nothing but an almost frozen breath that is still for a moment in the air. I belong to Him, and this is why I can withstand the hurled-down ice and the breath of God that freezes me at least for a season.

I cannot escape my new circumstances. Yet nothing can stop God's moments of reprieve. He doesn't take us out of the painful times, but He gives us breaks. I look at branches full of snow, and I understand how the weight of difficulties look different for all of us.

A Step Towards Life:

Take a walk in nature. Don't stay inside because of the rain or the snow. Whatever the weather may be, embrace it and walk. Engage your senses. What do you see? Is the sun touching your skin, or is it wet snow? Breathe deeply, smell, and taste. What sounds do you hear?

Take a photo and put it on social media or print it out and put it in a scrapbook. You might enjoy having a way to track your walks, your thoughts, or your prayers.

Intersections

"God is our refuge and strength, a very present help in trouble. Therefore we will not fear though the earth gives way, though the mountains be moved into the heart of the sea, though the waters roar and foam, though the mountains tremble at its swelling. There is a river whose streams make glad the city of God, the holy habitation of the Most High. God is in the midst of her; she shall not be moved, God will help her when morning dawns...

Be still and know that I am God..."

Psalm 46:1-5 and 46:10

A Note From My Journal:I am hardly awake as last night's memories resurface with deep regret. I want to run, but my eyes already see the devotional on my bedside table, so if I run, I'm blatantly looking at the face of God and turning, running away elsewhere, anywhere away from the presence of God.

It was a devotional sent with a Christmas card from my sister. Small and short. A verse followed by a couple of paragraphs. It was exactly what I needed.

I am always amazed when spiritual things intersect with the physical world. God meets us right where we are at any given moment. The December/January edition of *The Daily Bread*[4] was sitting on my

---

4 Our Daily Bread. Our Daily Bread Ministries, 1956–present.

bedside table. It was the size of a pamphlet I could hold in one hand, yet powerful and perfectly timed.

I was in the habit of buying a new devotional at the beginning of each year, but this year, I had not yet gotten around to it. My usual excitement for a new year was replaced with a sadness that I was finding hard to navigate. I didn't even know what to pray for or where to open my Bible. Sometimes, we are sick and weak and need the words of God to be served up gently by another person, like broth when we can't digest anything else but still need nourishment.

When the world around me was feeling hostile and unfamiliar, God gave me something familiar from my sister. I don't know how many times in my life just the right book for the next season of life was handed to me. It can sometimes be hard to notice these moments until we get still enough to reflect on the patterns God places on our lives. He is creative and original with each of us.

I found a pattern in my walk with Jesus. He spoke through books, words, and stories from childhood nights reading my grandmother's Guidepost magazines she had sequestered away in a bedside table drawer in her guest room. Not a word was wasted then or now.

When our ground shifts after divorce and we call out in prayer, we are not left alone. Maybe you can remember a time the spiritual world broke into your own physical life. God uses all creation to reach out to his beloved children. Music, trees, leaves, a painted canvas, a nurse's well-trained hand, stories told, and perfectly timed words read and applied to life's difficulties are all examples of how God reaches us. The created physical world collides with the invisible spiritual world and causes the expectant soul to feel something special.

A Step Towards Life:

All this creation ignites our senses, and then we realize we are not so alone after all. Seek out something created that speaks beautifully to you. A book, a piece of art, music-anything that inspires you. Be still and know that God is still God. You are still wonderfully and intricately made by the original Creator.

Take Thoughts Captive

"For though we walk in the flesh, we are not waging war according to the flesh. For the weapons of our warfare are not of the flesh but have divine power to destroy strongholds. We destroy arguments and every lofty opinion raised against the knowledge of God, and take every thought captive to obey Christ.."

2 Corinthians 10:3-5

A Note From My Journal: The beautiful thing about today is that I'm not rummaging around in a gun cabinet. I'm not crying (at least not yet). I'm back to being sober, and I'm pretty sure I would like to stay this way. When grief makes me lose my balance, I tend to reach for sharp, jagged edges that pierce instead of heal.

I have to stop leaning on the false things that look like help. My sadness is much too heavy to lean on anything but Jesus. The beautiful thing about today is I see a pathway that I never wanted to take, not through December, where expectations are high, nor through January, when I turned one year older. I look back at that forged pathway I walked through imperfectly and ungracefully, yet through. I'm still walking through.

I noticed as I went through the first months of being separated and living alone my thoughts became obsessive at times. One small thought upon which I ruminated could change the course of my day and quickly send me into a downward spiral. I was acting far differently from Paul's instructions: to destroy arguments and every lofty opinion raised against the knowledge of God and to take every thought captive.

The important thing to know is that you cannot trust every thought. Your thoughts produce your emotions. Neuroscientist Dr. Lee Warren says this, "...feelings aren't facts. Feelings just tell you that a certain set of physiological things are occurring in your body, and there may or may not actually be a threat."[5]

Physically, the body is producing a fight-or-flight hormone in hopes of saving your life. In the spiritual realm, the enemy is in a perfect position to attack your mind by bringing up every doubt about yourself and your relationships with others in your life, including your relationship with God.

If you are being attacked on both a physical and a spiritual level, please press pause. Take a few deep breaths or take a walk while prayerfully recalling the truth God has already revealed to you. You might need five seconds to declare some fiery dart of a word a lie. It can take several minutes to hold a thought captive and actually interrogate it for crossing your mind.

You might need an entire day or weekend to take one thought and consider it all the way through to a clear judgment. I hope you take whatever time frame you need to get your body settled down and your soul back in touch with the truth about who God is and who you really are. Remember how Satan attacked Eve in the Garden of Eden? He attacked her mind first. He said to the woman, "Did God actually say, 'You shall not eat of any tree in the garden'?" (Genesis 3:1).

---

5 Sprinkle, Preston, host. "The Brain, the Body, and Dealing with Trauma – Dr. Lee Warren." *Theology in the Raw*, 1 Mar. 2024, https://theologyintheraw.com/podcast/the-brain-the-body-and-dealing-with-trauma-dr-lee-warren/.

Imagine what could be avoided if we paused before accepting every thought our mind offered up or whatever thoughts from other people caused us pain. What if you filtered everything through the truth of who you are as a beloved child of God? Not every thought that barges into your mind needs to stay.

How many times has the enemy tried to convince you that you have misunderstood God's words? How many times has the enemy persuaded you into believing that what you already possess from God is not actually yours? Are you convinced that God is keeping wisdom, knowledge, and goodness from you? This is a convincing lie that distracts you from your own status as a beloved child of God who has the ability to communicate and understand your Creator. Secondly, this lie distracts us from God, the only one who loves perfectly and unwavering.

If part of my identity is having access to the mind of Christ, I need to pause and consider it, put it on as my own, and think through his mind, not my own. When I think of the mind of Christ, I feel strength. I can slow down no matter the busyness around me. The mind of Christ seems far away from the cacophony of differing opinions and the accusatory words of the enemy.

A Step Towards Life:

Pause and consider your thoughts as well as the emotions coming from them. Get a journal and write your thoughts so they are carefully contained on paper. Thoughts can now be examined from the perspective of being outside your mind instead of within.

A Calm, Cozy Space

"I will instruct you and teach you in the way you should go;
I will counsel you with my eye upon you.

Be not like a horse or a mule, without understanding,
which must be curbed with bit and bridle,
or it will not stay near you."
Psalm 32:8-9

A Note From My Journal: I prayed, "What does Your healing look like?"
This is what I find when I open the Bible to read: God's eye upon me.
Like the intimately acquainted friend with whom you can just make eye
contact across a crowded room and you both know it's time to go. I write
these verses beneath the title of my journal page: The Study of God. Do
I look my God in the eye? Do I follow His eyes and silently move in the
right direction? I think healing is here, in books and study and writing
these observations and reflections.

I'm not sure why, but when I first moved out, I craved smallness. The
world and my life seemed too big, complicated, and loud. Writing in
the pages of a journal I dedicated and named "The Days of the Rest
of My Life" brought me comfort.

It was a small space in which I could pour out thoughts that
needed to be safely processed. It's where I could record private moments of revelation. Without reflection, there is no growth. I would
ask myself questions like "Where am I?" and "Where do I want to

go?" A journal can be a way to release the emotions that threaten action. It is a calm space that invites you to be still and open up a new blank page that is waiting to be filled with all your anxious thoughts, prayers, and wonder at God's love and your life.

Even if it's a new thing for you to do, journaling is one of the most essential things you can do to help yourself through grief. Your thoughts will be released from your own mind and safely contained. Your journal can be as beautiful or as messy as you want it to be.

There are many ways to journal. There are prayer journals so we remember what we pray for and can identify the answer. A narrative journal is just telling your story and is a reflective way to understand exactly what is going on and how you really feel about it. A bullet journal will keep you organized. In Ryder Carrol's book, *The Bullet Journal Method*[6], he explains this popular way of keeping track of life.

Journaling has helped me process my thoughts, break down goals, and allowed for a brain dump whenever needed. I am more observant, intentional, and reflective as a journaler. Here are some reasons to add the practice of journaling to your life:

1. **Reduces anxiety.** Journaling can be a "brain dump" where you take all those random thoughts that seem to come to mind at inopportune times.

2. **Improves memory.** Grief can affect memory, and a lot happens during a separation and divorce. You can set aside a journal page for lists or notes on lawyer info, important conversation points, or ideas for moving or selling a house.

3. **Organization of your thoughts.** Pick one topic and write it

---

6 Carroll, Ryder. *The Bullet Journal Method: Track the Past, Order the Present, Design the Future.* Portfolio, 2018.

at the top of the page. Examples include: The Good Things I Can Pursue or 5 Things I'm Worried About And What Might Be A Possible Solution.

4. **Increases self-awareness.** A journal is a non-judgmental space to write out your true thoughts and feelings. Be as honest as you can be, and remember that no one else has to see your writing.

5. **Gain a new vision for your future.** This is especially true if you have been in a marriage for a long time. You might notice yourself on auto-pilot, doing things not necessarily because you want or need to but because it's something you did for your spouse that doesn't fit your life now.

6. **Record prayers and answers to prayers.** This helps your faith grow. Sometimes, we forget our prayers or hardly notice when a prayer is answered. By writing down our prayers and later making note of the answer, we become more spiritually skillful at seeing God's movement in our life.

7. **Lower stress:** Grief can be physically and emotionally taxing. Writing in a journal can be a form of self-care and stress relief. It provides an opportunity to release tension, reduce anxiety, and promote a sense of control in a situation that often feels chaotic and uncontrollable. The act of journaling can be calming and grounding.

8. **Improve communication skills:** Writing in a journal can enhance your communication skills by improving your ability to articulate thoughts and feelings. This can be beneficial in personal and professional relationships.

9. **Enhance sensitivity:** With practice, you will begin to notice when your senses are being engaged on a physical and spiritual level. We remember more when our senses are engaged, like the scent of rain as we take a walk.

10. **Inspire creativity:** We can write about things that inspire us to be who we desire to be. We can dream and come up with creative ways to handle difficulties as well as create a vision.

You can use fancy pens or markers, stickers, or stamps, but all you really need is a pen and a cheap notebook. There is something therapeutic about writing by hand, coloring, or doodling as you meditate and pour out your thoughts in ink. It reminds me of childhood, and I always feel better after a journaling session. There are some great YouTube videos about journaling. Most of them have a relaxing aesthetic and are just fun to watch and get ideas for your own therapeutic journaling experience.

Set up an atmosphere that is conducive to reflection and quiet thoughtfulness. Use soft music or simply light a scented candle to cue your mind that it is time to journal. Journaling is a transformative practice that has the remarkable ability to reshape our perspective on life. By putting pen to paper and documenting our thoughts, experiences, and emotions, we invite introspection and self-reflection into our daily lives.

This process of self-discovery enables us to step back from the chaos of everyday life and gain valuable insights into our beliefs, values, and goals. By regularly engaging in the act of journaling, we cultivate a heightened sense of self-awareness and develop a more objective view of our experiences. We begin to identify recurring patterns, recognize our strengths and weaknesses, and better comprehend the reasons behind our thoughts and behaviors. Journaling also serves as a powerful tool for processing emotions, as it allows us to navigate challenges and setbacks with greater resilience.

A Step Towards Life:

Develop a journaling ritual to reflect on how or when you felt the presence of spiritual guidance. Willingly divert your attention away from the busyness of the day; be still a few minutes or longer observe and reflect. Write it out and study what God is doing in your life.

A Time To Be Unapologetic

"Come to me all who labor and are heavy laden and
I will give you rest."

Matthew 11:18

A Note From My Journal: How do you come back after everything that has pressed pause on your life? You may have been kindly asked to leave the "House Of Mirth" because you don't seem to fit in anymore. You have become wearisome, and your tears make everyone feel awkward. They might say, "You are going to feel better later, and we will be here when you do."

It has only been six months, and my ex-husband is already dating. In the back of my mind, I consider maybe this is the same woman who left evidence behind for me to find. The months he tried to tell me nothing was going on, that I was paranoid, annoying, unaffectionate, and unlovable. He is already telling me to move on.

Don't apologize because something terrible happened and you need time to catch your breath. When someone pushes you beyond what you are ready to do says more about them than it does about you. Making others feel less guilty or less awkward is not your responsibility. You might find yourself receiving unwanted and unneeded advice from people who have their own plans.

I could sense my ex-husband's desire for me to move on. It was like he had a timeline for everything. When other people create chaos in our lives, and then they get angry when we react in a way they don't like, that is manipulation on their part. This is a time to be strong and stand up for yourself. Not motivated by revenge but motivated by the knowledge that God hates the injustice of divorce and the uneven measuring scales of measuring that come with it.

We have a responsibility to treat our lives like they matter. Don't give away what your loving God has given to you. Things like time to grieve and space to think. Don't be rushed into leaving your home or making decisions that will affect the rest of your life. Take your time, even if it doesn't fit into other people's timeline.

It's uncomfortable to be confrontational when you aren't used to being that way. A ten-minute confrontation telling someone what your own timeline looks like will be uncomfortable only for him a little while. But without the confrontation, you could be looking at months and maybe even years of discomfort.

Why apologize for the violence done toward your life? You don't owe words of explanation to anyone at all. God hates that divorce is happening to you. God hates when any cruel thing touches your life. Don't be confused; God is not saying He hates people that are divorced.

God hates it when his sons' and daughters' hearts break. God hates the divisiveness of what He meant for wholeness and holiness. God hates the lies and the lukewarm indifference where truth and wholehearted love should be.

Unapologetically step out of the confines of what God hates. Divorce is not who you are, and there is no apology needed. Whether it was you who initiated the divorce or your ex, it doesn't really matter. You have not failed because someone failed to love you.

A Step Towards Life:

We are meant to be like both animals Jesus described, the serpent as well as the dove. "I am sending you out as sheep in the midst of wolves, so be wise as serpents and innocent as doves" (Matthew 10:16). Sometimes, we have to strike to show a fiercer side of ourselves. Sometimes, we need to be gentle. Always, we need to be led by the Holy Spirit's wisdom. There is a time to unapologetically move forward in life at your own pace and in your own way. No approval is needed.

Faithful

"And behold, there came a voice to him and said,
"What are you doing here, Elijah?"

1 Kings 19:13

A Note From my Journal: The trees aren't still. I watch them as the wind blows against them. Sometimes, it is just a bare tree... limbs everywhere... naked and reaching for the winter sun. Like an infant, like an adult, like life sort of starting to explain why it exists in the first place. The air will be still again soon, and then the sun and stillness will warm and comfort me.

The most important thing to do at this moment is to do what feels faithful. Even if that is crying out, "Father." Letting tears fall and closing my eyes for a little sleep. The storm might be almost over...so I won't give up just yet. Instead, I'll be content one more minute because God is there, too, and that is a beautiful thing.

Why does my own name sound so jarring and unfamiliar coming from the man I loved? He started calling me by my first name. I know I can't be the only one that has experienced the strangeness of being called a term of endearment for years and then being so quickly renamed, even demoted in a sense.

Didn't we have three children? Didn't he use to say he adored me? But now he calls me JENNIFER. It makes me feel like I'm no longer home.

What am I doing here? Didn't God ask Elijah this same question?

"And he said, "Go out and stand on the mount before the Lord." And behold, the Lord passed by, and a great and strong wind tore the mountains and broke in pieces the rocks before the Lord, but the Lord was not in the wind. And after the wind an earthquake, but the Lord was not in the earthquake. And after the earthquake a fire, but the Lord was not in the fire. And after the fire the sound of a low whisper. And when Elijah heard it, he wrapped his face in his cloak and went out and stood at the entrance of the cave. And behold, there came a voice to him and said, "What are you doing here, Elijah?"

1 Kings 19:11-13

Elijah had been hiding in a cave. God gave him provision in food, water and rest. We can't stay hidden in caves. We can't remain terrified and timid, not when we know God *gave us a spirit not of fear but of power and love and self-control (1 Timothy 2:7).*

After our lives are shaken and blown about in the wind, after the storm and the fire, it's good for us to listen to the question God asks of us. But first, we step out of our own hiding place. Stand still and notice the ones who seek to harm us are not there.

What am I doing here? This place is no longer mine. It is no longer the place I feel at home. It was time to leave. It felt faithful to go where I was loved.

So that's what I did. I went to my parents' house, where they invited me, and I felt loved instead of rejected. I sat in a diner with my best friend for hours, talking without worry that my tears would scare her away, and actually, she brought the tissues. Connecting with others who loved me was like reaching for the warmth of the sun.

The warmth of others, when cold trauma shocks us, can steady us until we get our balance again. Don't deny yourself the connection of loved ones who want to be there for you. It's a reminder that you are still loved and appreciated.

You will find the people meant to be in your life. Don't be offended when some people let you go in favor of your ex. Just move on and know you will find the people who love and understand you. We don't need everyone to understand us.

A Step Towards Life:

Reaching out and responding to those people that offer friendship can comfort and support you. Having a face-to-face conversation allows you to safely share your thoughts and feelings. It is other people that can remind us of our own strengths and successes.

Stay grounded and rooted in the truth of God's words. Hold tight the friendship that provides you time and space to grieve. To whom might you reach out to? Pray about it and see who God brings to mind.

The Practice of Small

"Have you not known? Have you not heard?
The LORD is the everlasting God,
the Creator of the ends of the earth.
He does not faint or grow weary;
his understanding is unsearchable.

He gives power to the faint,
and to him who has no might he increases strength.
Even youths shall faint and be weary,
and young men shall fall exhausted;

but they who wait for the LORD shall renew their strength;
they shall mount up with wings like eagles;
they shall run and not be weary;
they shall walk and not faint."

Isaiah 40:28-31

A Note From My Journal: I need to work slow and unrushed from a place of abundance, not scarcity. Because God provides and keeps me safe, I do not need to strive for anything. I feel at peace each time I decide to stay right here and write.

I can thrive alone. It is actually the very essence of who I am. I am alone but free.

Often, it is the smallest steps we take in response to God's nurturing that aid us best. The practice of small steps seems to give me just enough momentum for one more step. I do know my Lord is the everlasting God. Time is nothing to Him, and the idea of living and working and figuring out my way through grief in a dimension that has no timeline at all gives me relief.

Small strides faithfully walked out day by day gets us closer to the end we seek. One moment at a time, our lives are bound up like a book. A step toward life by the grace of God can land us safe and sound exactly where we are meant to be. A refreshed, healing life awaits us as we put one bare foot down on the floor and step out of the bed we would rather stay in because stress and sadness make us exhausted.

Maybe the small step is just a cup of coffee on a cold winter morning, but even this is a small blessing to be thankful for. As you feel your feet on the floor, smell the scent of coffee, and notice the morning sun illuminate the frost on leaves, you can whisper words of gratitude to God. It is in this noticing stance that the joy of the Lord is ours. The joy of the Lord gives us strength. Do you notice the small everyday moments? These are lifelines that slow us down and allow us the opportunity to wait on God to renew our strength.

We can wait. We need to wait because the alternative is too much. The alternative is rushing our body always onward while our soul faints within. I know for me, when I feel my soul fainting, I lose my senses as well as what I believe to be the Holy Spirit guiding me.

I stop noticing the touch of solid ground and the scents that bring comfort. My eyesight doesn't notice beauty but tends to fade all beauty out. There is no practice of small. There is no rest or renewal.

Life can be severely altered during and after a divorce. I fainted often and failed at things I had set out to do for the day in my work as well as my personal life. I saw things I'd worked hard at for years crumble. When I felt weak, I did, at times, reach for things I knew were unhealthy for me. Old habits that were once conquered offered up deceivingly beautiful escapes.

When I did fail or faint I knew God rescued me. He never left me with that emptiness the way the so- called beautiful escapes always did. I prayed for help and I prayed for comfort. I had no idea how God would do either, but He always came through. It was never a big dramatic thing. His rescue was in small, quiet, delicate things that might not be noticed by anyone else.

You may feel hopeless, as if you will never run again,
> " …they shall run and not be weary;
> they shall walk and not faint."

Isaiah 40:31b

God promises you help when you wait on him,
> "but they who wait for the LORD shall renew
> their strength;
> they shall mount up with wings like eagles…"

Isaiah 40:31a

You might imagine waiting on God as sitting still and doing nothing, but waiting on God is a very active shifting of your mind and setting of your will. The Hebrew word for waiting is Qavah: To wait, to hope, to bind together. Waiting on God is an expectation that He is already rescuing us. We get to take a moment to catch up on how and where God is inviting us to join Him.

In waiting on God, we actively hope in the love and providence that knits us together, tightly binding us for the road ahead. God with us is what renews us and gives us the strength we need to soar like eagles.

We let striving go by the wayside while waiting on God. Striving and manipulating circumstances for our own agenda robs us of everything truly abundant for our soul. In waiting for God, we get to see Him in the small details that have meaning to us. For me, leaves with frost, the scent of coffee, working slowly instead of feeling rushed, these are small things God gives me joy in.

I can practice noticing these things every day. I believe God will show me more as we journey together all the way through every aspect of life.

A Step Towards Life:

Journal about your own practice of small. Reflect on the things that bring you joy in the midst of even your saddest moments. Which of the five senses do you experience? Maybe there are small things that have gone unnoticed as being from the God who created you and knows you the most. Start to journal and keep track of the small things that minister to your body and soul.

What Remains

"No longer do I call you servants, for the servant does not know what his master is doing; but I have called you friends, for all that I have heard from my Father I have made known to you."

John 15:15

A Note From My Journal: Who I once loved is now unrecognizable. It's a strange place to be in trying to be friends, but honestly, in the back of my mind, I am not hopeless that the man I loved and still love... because can anyone just stop loving on demand.. ..might find his love for me again. Hatred and love aren't opposites. I understand that now. I'm finding that what hurts the most is the indifference, not love nor hate, just some generic weak try at remaining friends to ease a guilty conscience. Honestly, it's not friendship at all. It's just me walking into betrayal over and over again.

I cut my visit with my dad short and drove back home to the house into which I'd recently moved. I was shocked to see half a tree on the roof and a lilac bush that looked as if it had been pulled up from the ground, roots and all. There were a few trees down, and others looked broken-limbed but still standing. My tree-lined yard looked rough. Inside, the house seemed fine. There were no broken windows and no water dripping from the ceiling.

When we are faced with devastating things, it is a good idea to stop and assess the damage done and what is left. What are dangerous things that only injure us more when we cling to them? What remains that can be picked up out of the rubble, cleaned up, and made new? What do I desperately desire to remain, but in reality, no amount of cleanup will ever repair it?

An example was trying to remain friends with my ex-husband. I tried but failed over and over. I'm glad I tried because it is a blessing to know that I didn't go without a fight to save something. But the person who injured you is not the person who is capable of aiding in any healing.

We need to assess what actually remains. We remove the broken, dangerous pieces. We try to repair until we realize no amount of genuine kindness is going to change someone else or heal our own grief.

When we look at life after the storm, the fire, the death, and devastation, it's the silent audacity of the day going on with its blue skies and sunshine that feels like a shock. It feels too fast, too loud, and too bright because I'm not ready to avert my eyes from the damage yet. My mind is not settled on the next rational step yet.

Make efforts to distance yourself as much as you can from your ex, as well as people who aren't allowing you to go through the grief process. Make an intentional pivot with your mind and body. Look at your marriage honestly. Face the good and the bad. When we face our truth about ourselves, as well as about others, we are freed to walk forward in one intentional direction.

Here are some questions to journal about that may be helpful in deciding what remains in truth and what only remains in our futile attempts to repair something irreparable and dangerous to us. Spend some time journaling and meditating on these questions and see what path God may be guiding you toward.

+ What exactly happened? Just like with a natural disaster, you need to know what exactly caused the damage in full or in part. Damage from a tornado will need a different set of tools to clean up than a fire or a flood.

+ What part did each person play in the damage done? Include your own faults and shortcomings.

+ Shift your thought process more towards yourself (who you can change) and away from the person causing the hurt (who you cannot change). Ask yourself, what are some harbored disobediences that God has placed on your heart to consider? What is one step you can take immediately to get back into an intimate relationship with God?

+ What do you think God wants to remove from your life? What is never to be resurrected again?

+ How would it feel to let go of shame and unforgiveness and grasp onto mercy for yourself and grace for others?

God tells us not to lie. Lying to ourselves about our own state of being as well as the state of others is still a lie, and there is no freedom in that space.

A Step Towards Life:

It will take time, and energy, and maybe money to clean up the damage done to your life, but God is a master of creating new and beautiful lives. It is comforting to know through storms of all kinds that Jesus is the one friend that never grows tired. He is never too busy to hear our prayers and walk us through devastating things. His energy fills us, and his providence has no bounds.

Jesus offers faith when we are full of fear. We get to decide whether fear or faith will dictate our life. I know it's excruciatingly hard to let go of the broken things and walk empty-handed until

Jesus gives you something whole to hold onto. There may be days of discomfort, days spent in vain trying to put things back together, but the best thing we can do is tell ourselves the truth about what actually remains.

The Restoring Love of God

"I will restore to you the years
that the swarming locust has eaten,
the hopper, the destroyer, and the cutter,
my great army, which I sent among you.

"You shall eat in plenty and be satisfied,
and praise the name of the LORD your God,
who has dealt wondrously with you.
And my people shall never again be put to shame."

Joel 2:25-26

A Note From My Journal: I must accept my marriage is over. The temptation to dwell on what I wasted instead of cherishing is strong. I need to get on with the legal and living arrangements. My thoughts and emotions are having a difficult time keeping up through this divorce process. Forgive me and restore me. I need your help.

When I pray for forgiveness, it is because I have entertained misleading thoughts for too long. The truth is that I gave up too much for the man I loved. This is a lesson learned, not exactly a waste, even though it sometimes felt like it. It wasn't all a waste of time and energy.

I know now that failure teaches us how we shouldn't do things and helps us understand how we would like or not like to live. We fail at specific points in our marriage, not the whole marriage. It's unhelpful to take a marriage and deem it rotten and a complete failure.

There had to have been things in the marriage that worked.

My marriage wasn't a waste, and neither was yours. It would be a waste to now live as if you didn't still have a whole life ahead of you. If divorce is my destiny, I will not try to get out of it. It is not in my control to force someone to love me; actually, it would be cruel and wrong to manipulate circumstances for what I want. A love that exists only one-sided or forced is not actual love but a perversion of it.

If we live in God's love, we get to witness God turning something meant to harm us into something good and beneficial to us. What we lose, God can restore, or like Joel 2:25 states, "I will restore to you the years that the swarming locust has eaten..."

Sometimes, others betray us, steal from us, and eat away at our lives. Look at Joseph, sold into slavery by his brothers. Many years later, Joseph was in the position to feed these same brothers when they came to Egypt to find food during a famine in their own land. Joseph recognizes them, gives them food, and says, "As for you, you meant evil against me, but God meant it for good, to bring it about that many people should be kept alive, as they are today" (Genesis 50:20).

God changes things. He turns things to move in completely new directions. Someone else's plans to harm you might leave you feeling betrayed and unlovable, but the moment you shift your thoughts to curiosity in what God is doing, you are one step closer to taking back your own life and giving God the glory for it.

A Step Towards Life:

Meditate on the verses Joel 2:25-26, Genesis 50, and Romans 8:28. Compare your thoughts on restoration and God's thoughts on restoration in these verses. The circumstances we face aren't meant to destroy us in God's eyes, but we have an enemy whose motivation is to kill, steal, and destroy us. God will rescue and restore us.

Our True Power

"If the Spirit of him who raised Jesus from the dead dwells in you, he who raised Christ Jesus from the dead will also give life to your mortal bodies through his Spirit who dwells in you."

Romans 8:11

A Note From My Journal: I feel my soul settling down from the uproar. I see the pieces of my life that were thrown up into the air settle into spaces that are new and clear. Pieces of my life that seemed dangerously unsettled now feel safer. Safe new spaces are settling while other pieces of my life float further away. All the crashed and smashed pieces are lying in a rubble pile that I know I need to leave behind and not even keep a shard of for memory's sake. But the pieces I get to keep and the spaces I can still indwell are womanhood, motherhood, observing life, being a teacher, being a writer, and being a businesswoman. All this is still mine.

The same storm that uprooted my lilac bush and caused half a tree to fall on my roof is not going to gently replant or remove fallen branches. Someone with the right tools and knowledge will be needed to clear away and clean up the damage. I know how tempting it is to sit and dwell on the rubble, but I promise it's not worth it. You only do more damage and hurt yourself further.

Assessing the damage done is closely related to beginning to accept, especially if you have the mindset that your life could be a brand new start. Trust me, there are some great things about being divorced. There is still a future and a hope. It might just not be in sight yet, and it might look different than you imagined.

Imagine the power it would take to raise the dead. Imagine the power that removed my lilac tree right out of the ground and left it unplanted lying, on the ground half-dead. We know God uses nature to move mountains and lift up trees through his mighty power. We know work becomes easier when we pick up the right tools and apply them to one specific goal.

The correct tool does nothing until we pick it up and use it. The same thing goes with the power of God within us. If you are a Christian, you already have this power living in you. If you are not a Christian, it's only a matter of becoming a Christian that allows you access to such power. We may have power, but are we actually utilizing it?

We make strides ahead when we find the right tools, and we have faith enough to access the power in our lives. In rebuilding, we must recognize the power we have and use it instead of letting it remain dormant. You are still alive. You are free.

God's power cannot be confined. When we allow the Holy Spirit to nudge us with questions that need honest answers, it is the hand of God reaching out to you. God may ask you completely different questions from the ones above. Pray and be prepared to answer Him. Remember this when questions make you well up with tears:

> "For I am sure that neither death nor life, nor angels nor rulers, nor things present nor things to come, nor powers, nor height nor depth, nor anything else in all creation, will be able to separate us from the love of God in Christ Jesus our Lord."
>
> Romans 8:38-39

Our God never leaves us. The power is plugged in when we place our own life right into his hands.

A Step Towards Life:

What would it look like if you didn't just remember God's Spirit is within you, but you acted upon it? Consider the real question. It isn't "Am I able?" but "Am I willing?"

Have a Vision and Set a Goal

"If people can't see what God is doing,
they stumble all over themselves;
But when they attend to what he reveals,
they are most blessed."

Proverb 29:18, MSG

Note From My Journal: Some Goals:

1. Get stable. My mind, my body, my spirit.

2. Be disciplined (because my life depends on it).

A friend of mine was talking about how we act surprised, as if things just suddenly happen. We act as if we have forgotten God is always creating and working behind the scenes. God has gone before us. Where I see the dark void, God is there, hovering over me like a highly skilled surgeon.

Wisdom hands the surgeon the knife to cut out what doesn't belong. I lay on a table, counting backward out loud until I'm unconscious. Prudence signals now, right now. Cut, pluck them out, or cauterize the wound because no time is left.

It's like the beginning all over again on repeat for eternity. God, with wisdom and prudence, looks at what is a reality and carefully, knowingly, removes the unhealthy and restores health to us. God looked at the dark void and formed earth, oceans, skies, and human life. If God can envision all of creation with its every intricate detail, why do we assume He cannot transform our personal darkness and chaos into something teeming with light and creativity?

A vision comes first. Wisdom is called upon second. Wisdom is the ability to think and act according to knowledge. If we lack the knowledge, ask for it, and God will provide it. Prudence is the careful procedures needing to be done in order to bring the vision to light.

"I, wisdom, dwell with prudence, and I find knowledge and discretion."

Proverbs 8:12

Prudence is the surgery, the cutting away of the unhealthy, as well as setting the healthy up for survival. Maybe this is what we don't see or can't see at times. We don't know all the steps yet. This is the difference between having a vision and a goal.

Vision is deciding that you want an area or aspect of your life to look and feel a certain way. It's like envisioning a perfectly planned day. Vision gives us hope. Without vision, we are stuck in an unhealthy state of passivity. Vision dictates goals.

How we develop vision is different for all of us, but one thing we have in common is using our creativity. Try to look at something, a piece of old furniture, an empty room, or a difficult situation, and then ask yourself, "What is one thing I could add or take away to change the status of one of these?" When we ask a question like this, the answer is dependent upon what we value as an individual. An example would be if you value classic carpentry and recognize a piece of furniture as having good bones, then you might sand the piece down and restain it. If you value more modern and sleek furniture, you might remove the vintage knobs and put them on a more modern piece.

It is important to know your own values and your purpose behind doing what you do. Having a clear vision keeps us in touch with our own personal integrity. We can set goals now to get us closer to the image we have in our mind- the vision. We can pull out our calendars and write down the steps each day to get us closer to what we desire.

When we set goals and then implement each step, we gain confidence in our ability to create something out of very little or nothing at all. Start with a small goal if you feel overwhelmed. Be specific about the goal. Say your vision is being energetic, healthy, and fit. Your goal for Monday might be at 4:00pm you walk a mile, and then you stretch. Picture yourself doing this. What are you wearing? What if it rains? What can you do after? Set yourself up for success by answering these questions and being specific rather than vague and slightly undecided.

A Step Towards Life:

This is an exercise where journaling will be helpful in reminding you of your values. Sometimes, emotions obscure our vision, and unhelpful thoughts discourage us from stepping boldly out in the direction we need to go. You can look at this list of your own values and principles that you desire to live by, like an inner compass. These are your values gained from your experiences, knowledge, and wisdom, not the expectations of others.

Don't say you value something when you really don't but you are convinced you should. Be honest with yourself. What do you value? Here are some of my personal values as an example:

1. Self-Confidence
2. Growth and well-being
3. Freedom and independence

Now think about your own values. What can you do to live within the boundaries of your values?

Look at your life and try to develop a vision. Use your wisdom and the knowledge you have and prudently apply it to the delicate steps needed to reach the goal from sickness to wellness.

Fading

"A voice says, "Cry!"
And I said, "What shall I cry?"
All flesh is grass,
and all its beauty is like the flower of the field.
The grass withers, the flower fades
when the breath of the LORD blows on it;
surely the people are grass.
The grass withers, the flower fades,
but the word of our God will stand forever."

Isaiah 40:6-8

A Note From My Journal: Dear God, I will not give Your gifts away for nothing. I pray for the wisdom to discern what fades away because it was never eternal in the first place, and what is meant for me, maybe not eternal but lifegiving to my eternal soul.

About a month after the storm hit my house, my yard flooded, knocking down a fence and filling my basement with just enough water to make me fear that I made a terrible decision in buying it. Seeing water that looks like a rushing river through your backyard is terrifying. So I panicked. I made some quick decisions about moving. I started to look into the process of selling the house.

I had never lived on my own alone or been responsible for everything pertaining to a house. My first thought was I absolutely had to move. I spent a weekend looking at places to rent closer to a bigger city, which I sort of wanted anyway but just hadn't gotten the courage up for. I wondered if this was a nudge from the Holy Spirit. Or was it overreaction and panic?

I rashly took off on a Tuesday morning after the flooding. I drove an hour away to the wooded land I still owned. I didn't exactly know why. I just felt I had to go there and walk again.

I walked down a familiar path of gravel and looked at my area of land for the first time in a year and a half. The land was completely grown over with thickets, thorns, and tall grass. It was so quiet and peaceful. I walked and breathed and remembered how my life used to revolve around walking and photographing each season of this place.

This felt like home. Home and a sense of belonging anywhere was a difficulty I faced and sort of accepted as the wife of a Marine. This was supposed to be where we were finally home together. But now the land was split, and the house we used to live in had been turned into a hunting cabin.

I felt a shift in my perspective as I walked that day in the August heat while wildflowers leaned because it was almost time for their blooms to fade and die. It seemed symbolic in so many ways. There is that unexplainable way our Creator changes our minds to see what couldn't have been seen before that very moment. My heart released, and I felt free.

I cried as I walked past wildflowers, not because I was sad but because I remembered the happiness I had felt when I was living there, picking flowers every week and making bouquets. It sounds so small. How could walks and picking wildflowers mean so much? It was getting to know the land in the years I lived there.

The expectation of the daisy and the daffodil every spring. The goldenrod in Fall. The evergreen and blue juniper berries in the winter. Nature was my decor.

It started to dawn upon me that fading away isn't bad or worse than but simply neutral and different. The land was still there, and it was still mine. My attention or lack of attention to the land never changed its existence. I neglected it because I lacked courage to act like its owner.

My ex-husband's cruel words challenged me, "How would you even take care of this place if it was yours?" He asked at the beginning of the separating process. I wanted to stay there, but I ended up negotiating to own a portion of the land, and I moved away. It was unbelievably sad to lose not only my marriage but also my home and the majority of the land.

I still stood in the August heat with the knowledge of God's love and power over my life. I knew in my heart that, yes, there are things that naturally fade away, like human love and seasons of life, but there are still beautiful gifts from God that need to be accepted, held tightly, and celebrated.

A Step Towards Life:

God has his ways of opening our spiritual eyes to the truths that eventually set us free. If we ask for the truth to be revealed, He will reveal it if you are searching with a pure heart. Being aware of yourself and the presence of God paves the way for a clearer perspective of what is naturally fading away. Make a list of what is fading or changing. Make another list of what God reveals to you as things that need to be held onto as precious and yours.

Self-Awareness that Gives Us God-Awareness

"I do not ask that you take them out of the world, but that you keep them from the evil one. They are not of the world, just as I am not of the world. Sanctify them in the truth; your word is truth. As you sent me into the world, so I have sent them into the world. And for their sake, I consecrate myself, that they also may be sanctified in truth."

John 17:15-19

A Note From My Journal:I feel chaos and overwhelm so easily. Tell me again and again that You are guiding me. Tell me this way and not that way. Remind me of only the essential one good thing for each moment. I forget myself so often. You know how I get lost because there is no compass in my head.

I believe wholeheartedly that, often, it is not new information we need but to be reminded of what we already know we need to do: know God, know ourselves, and know others.

I am still here and still alive because God isn't done with my soul. God is still revealing Himself. He is showing me the ways our images align. Not in every way, of course, but when I notice who God is it gives me clues of who I am. If I have enough knowledge of God to be able to trust and to obey, I begin the journey to wisdom (Proverbs 9:10).

Our self-image can become so clouded as we experience divorce. The world around us, the ex, and even our own thoughts can cause our awareness to be clouded. So, how does this journey of wisdom begin, and how do we continue onward once we've started on the path? We continue by abiding with God.

We abide with Him by walking with Him through this world we are not yet meant to leave. The created and the Creator can walk hand in hand through the chaos and overwhelm that the many distractions of the world around us offer. God never seems like He is in a hurry. When He stops, we need to stop and abide with Him.

Pour your thoughts out to Him. Pray his promises back to Him because as you do so, your respect for Him grows. In this practice, we know He hears us and listens to us. As He reminds you of all that you are, remind Him that you also know all that He is.

Self-awareness is not a selfish attitude; it is actually the opposite. It's facing the truth of who you really are and why you do the things you do. It's an ability to honestly assess your real strengths and your real weaknesses. Self-awareness is knowledge of your own character, feelings, and motivations.

Think about how Jesus Christ knew exactly who He was and why He did the things He did. The story of Jesus at twelve staying behind in the temple without His parents knowledge clearly reveals Jesus had self-awareness and did not doubt it:

> "And when his parents saw him, they were astonished. And his mother said to him, 'Son, why have you treated us so? Behold, your father and I have been searching for you in great distress.' And he said to them, 'Why were you looking for me? Did you not know that I must be in my Father's house?'"
>
> Luke 2:48-49

When we are self-aware, we develop the ability to pull the truth out of the lies. Mary accused Jesus of causing her and Joseph distress. The truth is Jesus didn't distress them. Mary just forgot who Jesus was, and this caused her and Joseph distress. Jesus had to remind them of who He really was and why He was there in the first place.

Have you ever wondered how you could feel so in touch and peaceful as you read the Bible and pray during a morning quiet time, but within an hour of getting up and entering into the work of the day, you lose that peace? You might lose your temper with someone or feel a deep sense of anxiety about something. Something I find helpful is remembering my own bent towards certain things. Knowing my own personality traits clues me in on where I may need help.

Knowing what to ask God saves us time and energy we might otherwise waste on stubbornly trying to do it all by ourselves. Asking God is a sign of belief in Him. God knows what we are capable of; otherwise, we wouldn't be here. Jesus prayed it best in John 17:15. We aren't taken out of the world but helped through it.

We are told to pray without ceasing. A way to do this is by having a continual inner dialogue, asking for what you need, and offering praise for the good that we experience. Abiding isn't just the state you are in when you purposely set aside time each morning to pray and read the Bible. Abiding is remaining mindful of Him throughout your everyday tasks. The mindset that can alter the perspective the most is that there is no separation between the areas of our lives; one area holy and another area secular. God doesn't leave us when we start our daily work. All of life can be holy when we seek to please God in every area of life.

A Step Towards Life:

Abide quietly with God. Do something where your mind can wander. A walk, washing the dishes, working on embroidery or just laying down for a few minutes could all get you into a posture of abiding. Think about what God could be trying to remind you of about Himself or about yourself.

What is true about you? Have you been misunderstood simply because you are being exactly who God created you to be? Pray and meditate upon what comes up for you.

Use What You Have

"Look at the birds of the air: they neither sow nor reap nor gather into barns, and yet your heavenly Father feeds them. Are you not of more value than they? And which of you by being anxious can add a single hour to his span of life?"

Matthew 6:26-27

A Note From My Journal: Why am I suffering? Is Jesus sitting at the well with no bucket to draw water? Is Jesus amidst 5,000 hungry people with no resources to feed? I point out ever so prayerfully all I lack and all I need. I want to save the little I have because the rest of my life looms ahead…I am calling it being responsible and saving, but really, it's responding to God with a no thank you, and I'll just bury my treasure down deep to save, but save until when? Because today I'm alive. Today, I need some joy, but I deny myself all of it due to fear.

———

In my own way, I was saying, "Lord, this chunk of money I gained from this divorce is all I have, and I need to save it for my future." This sounds responsible, and for some people, maybe it would be. But my personal Savior knew my heart and my thoughts. Thoughts of fear and anxiety, and thoughts that were steeped in human scarcity.

I had been praying for a new place to live or for a change of heart where I was living if he wanted me to stay. I felt miserable where I was. I had lost too much. Yet, I would not even consider using the money I had set aside to save for the future. A few other people mentioned I could use it, but I never considered it.

It is so easy to be deceived into trusting in money, jobs, people, and our own abilities. I went months thinking I was doing what was right by keeping that money and finding other ways to make myself happy. But God was trying to show me something. I was constantly repairing and spending money on the house I had recently moved into. I was spending money on a place where I didn't want to be. I felt trapped, overwhelmed, and extremely isolated.

I thought moving out of the house I shared with my husband was the best idea at the time, and he was more than willing to help me move out. I was hurting and wanted to flee, so I did. A new house in a new town seemed like it might be a good idea, but the reality set in quickly. My life was not a Hallmark movie. But I just kept trying to make it work.

I failed over and over because the truth was the things I enjoyed most were at least an hour or two drive away. No fitness classes, bookstores, or coffee shops, and very little beauty surrounded me. I did make a few friends, and for that, I'm thankful. It was obvious I was leaning upon my ability to make things work out no matter what.

I was settling for good enough. Once again, I was falling into an old habit of ignoring my true desires. I was spending on cheap imitations, trying to keep my soul satisfied on what did not really feed me in any way. I had to answer the question one morning as I read and meditated on Isaiah 55:2:

> "Why do you spend your money for that which is not bread, and your labor for that which does not satisfy? Listen diligently to me, and eat what is good, and delight yourselves in rich food."

Jesus was offering me cold water that would satisfy, and I was responding like the woman at the well (John 4:11). I was telling Jesus I didn't think He could draw out the best and everlasting water.

My human eyes thought Jesus lacked the tools. These verses cleared my vision.

Why was I walking on streets lined with cars when I had land with trees and water and wildflowers? I was spending my resources on something that didn't nourish my soul. I hated this new place I had rashly moved to. I was in a scarcity mindset that was causing me to hoard what I had instead of thanking God for what I did have in reality, but I was too fearful to use and enjoy. God was offering me what my soul needed most, and I was too busy trying to convince myself that the desire to simply live on my land again and walk in the woods was too small of a reason.

Why do any of us settle for less than what Christ offers? He ministers to the depths of our soul. He offers abundance, but we so often question the ministering hand and judge it wasteful or unwise. We so often have exactly what we need or want but don't use it.

I need to be reminded often that if I don't have, it's because I haven't asked (James 4:2). I have to ask God with my whole heart and trust my own mind and heart to discern what He reveals to me as an answer to my need or want. There is asking and searching that needs to be followed up with expectation and recognition of an answer.

I need to recognize the answer as the voice of God and use what God provides. My soul needed the wildflowers, even if they seemed insignificant. Jesus said:

> "Look at the birds of the air: they neither sow nor reap nor gather into barns, and yet your heavenly Father feeds them. Are you not of more value than they? And which of you

by being anxious can add a single hour to his span of life?" (Matthew 6:26).

A Step Towards Life:

Admit where you are coming from; is it fear? An abundant mindset or one of lacking and hoarding up? Is it a quiet and confident spirit? Consider what your life might look like if you knew wholeheartedly that all providence comes from God caring for you, not your own attempts to nourish yourself.

Detachment and Attachment

"If anyone comes to me and does not hate his own father and mother and wife and children and brothers and sisters, yes, and even his own life, he cannot be my disciple."

Luke 14:26

A Note From My Journal:My work right now is removing my love, my concern, my desire, and giving it all to God instead. I have to let him go. We are toxic together. I've known that for a long time....if we are ever friends again, it will have to be brand new, built on something other than leftover emotion from a marriage. We have been friends since we were 14. So how sad to have absolutely nothing of each other anymore.

Growing up, I thought we needed attachment. I thought that being detached was being distant from others or living apart from the world around me. Detachment seemed to be a sort of depressed state of being. But the truth is, more that a detached person is not externally detached but internally detached. They are doing exactly what they were put on earth to do in their sphere of influence, yet this outside world comes second to their inner world, where Christ and relationship with God comes before anything else.

I had been reading the book *The Way of Perfection* by St. Teresa of Avila[7], the 16th-century Carmelite nun. She introduced a whole new unexplored side of detachment to me. My first thought was, why be detached? Wouldn't this be a negative thing?

In her book, she explains that we should tear our hearts away from everything else; then seek God and we will surely find him.

Tear your heart away from everything else. It isn't hating. It is the process of knowing the goal but remaining unbothered by any obstacle or outcome. Detachment is when we let go of our own expectations of the future and embrace the reality of the here and now.

Attachment causes us to cling to our own interests and expectations of how any given part of life should be. Detachment is an unrushed attitude because, in a way, we don't care about the outcome. We trust in God's power and sovereignty, and it's quite possible we don't know God's actual plan or whole plan, so we are free to do only what God has clearly set as a goal for us alone.

Jesus explains that if we cannot hate our mother and father, husband or wife, brother or sister, and even our own life, we cannot be his disciples (Luke 14:26). I often wondered about this verse growing up. I didn't always quite understand it, but I heard an explanation from a pastor that made sense to me. The verse is more about the comparison of our love and desire for Christ being so much greater than our love and desire for a human relationship, a career, or anything else that can potentially become more loved than God.

St. Teresa talks about detachment from family, and it sounds severe for our day and time, but it makes sense that we should be able to detach ourselves from any created thing or being. To "tear

---

7 St. Teresa of Avila. *The Way of Perfection*. Dover, 2012. Originally published by Sheed and Ward, 1946.

your hearts away" sounds violent and difficult. But Jesus says there is a time for this kind of detachment. When we can no longer live close to Christ because someone else or something else has become more important or more influential than God Himself, then it is a good time to consider the choice to follow Christ and detach from whatever He has made known to us to lay down so we can walk with Him in full peace and joy.

How do we detach? Saint Teresa talks about how humility cannot exist without love, and love cannot exist without humility. It is impossible for these virtues to exist except where there is great detachment from all created things.

We need to pursue humility to detach from people and circumstances. A first step is admitting to ourselves that someone or something seems to easily offend us. None of us like to admit that we are bothered. But that is pride and only sets you up for a weaker state of being. Don't negotiate with your thoughts that may be lying about the situation or person. Remember, our thoughts do not always tell us the truth.

I think we desire detachment, but we get so addicted to the momentary dopamine hit that results from other people's approval. There is no getting around the fact that if we value one attachment, then we must detach from other attachments that encroach upon a healthy boundary. Developing our own boundaries is an important process. Our attention and love cannot go to everyone or everything.

After divorce, boundaries are needed not just within the breaking up of the relationship but also with what we tolerate from other people who may not be giving us the space we need. At times, it will be better for us to simply stay quiet and not involve ourselves with certain people, conversations, or things. Detach from what isn't good for you and attach instead to what feels like guarding your heart.

Try an exercise in detachment. Write in your journal at the top of a page this Proverb, "Above all else, guard your heart for everything you do flows from it" (Proverbs 4:23, NIV).

Shut the journal and go about your day. Stay mindful and notice moments when someone else's words or actions bring up an emotional response, like anger or sadness. Since our thoughts produce our emotions, ask yourself, "What am I letting these actions or words mean to me? How is my mind reasoning out this situation?"

Just because a divorce feels like rejection and your identity feels stolen doesn't mean these things are true. Protect your own heart by letting it safely rest while you examine and think on what you know to be true. Open your journal and write down the truth you understand about yourself, about God, about the people or circumstances that are encroaching upon your heart and mind in unhealthy ways. These are the truths that guard your heart.

A Step Towards Life:

Instead of an emotional reaction, imagine yourself remaining detached. Step away for a minute. Take a deep breath and get outside of yourself. Take notice and decide if a boundary is being crossed or maybe a boundary needs to be put in place. What is being offered up to you through someone else's actions or words? Decide for yourself if it needs to be accepted or denied.

My Eyes and God's Eyes

"Do not say, 'I will repay evil';
wait for the Lord, and he will deliver you.
Unequal weights are an abomination to the Lord,
and false scales are not good."

Proverbs 20:22-23

A Note From My Journal: I know it was God that let me find out about the affair. The note, the perfume, the Christmas ornament clearly stating they would be together by next Christmas. I'm glad I know. God's rescue can look like unwilling eyes being pried open.

I felt extremely rushed to move out, to start a new life somewhere else. He packaged it up all nicely and neatly, and naively, I still believed he had my best interest in mind. His seemingly helpful ways were really just about moving me out of his life and our home.

It was naive of me because as soon as the divorce papers were signed, his promised friendship and respect for me as the mother of his children disappeared completely. He always had a timeline. I see that now. Everyone told me I was being too nice and giving too much up, but I thought that for us, it could be amicable and friendly. But in the end, it was neither.

In the end, I realized how much I had been lied to, used up, and manipulated into thinking it was my own fault that he rescinded his promises. My emotional responses were completely natural, given the grief I was going through. Grief he used against me. I tried to explain to him, but I was always cut off abruptly. I had so many questions. The injustice infuriated me.

Did he ever love me? How long had he been trying to love me but just couldn't? Was he seeking revenge for something I'd done in the past? I no longer knew this person or even liked this person, which felt wrong because I still loved and adored our children.

Why in the world was I still trying to explain myself? One morning, as I walked around a lake, I was admiring purple clusters of flowers on the bank. As I looked, a soft-sounding question came to mind. "Can you give this person up?" and then the deeper question, "What if this is God saving my life?"

I walked on and thought about this. If I knew it was God doing something in my life, even if it was hard and hurting me, it would be easier to accept. If it is God who loves me and turns every evil thing into something that ends up benefiting me, then this divorce was walking me closer to a deeper and more intimate relationship with my Creator. This is the same God that only gives good gifts to his children.

God didn't give me the divorce. God doesn't cause hurt and death. God walks us through the evil and messed up things in life. He opens our eyes to the truth even when people desperately try to hide it.

God hates the lies and injustice that turn our lives into chaos. If I take my eyes off the injustice of the person who is causing the hurt and losses, I'm now free to look right into the eyes of God, and my perspective changes. I am detached from all the things that are, in the end, meaningless, and I become attached to the one and only person who can fully know and love me unconditionally.

It isn't for us to make sure someone pays the price for injustice. A focus on revenge will only cause us to become bitter and blind towards all else that has the potential to be good for us. God sees you and hears your prayers. Let God alone rescue you.

A Step Towards Life:

Meditate on these questions: What might change for you if you began practicing the belief that God hates injustice and unfairness? He knows exactly the evil that is touching your life and He is in complete control. Maybe a weight would be lifted off of you. Recognize the wrong done but don't remain focused on it. Focus on where and how God is walking, working and sharing truth with you.

Rethinking Loneliness

"Behold, the hour is coming, indeed it has come, when you will be scattered, each to his own home, and will leave me alone. Yet I am not alone, for the Father is with me."

John 16:32

A Note From My Journal:

A prayer to point us home "Into your hands I commit my spirit..." Psalm 31:5 Jesus added, "Father." Father, You are the Lord God that introduced yourself to Moses as I AM Who I AM- Yahweh. When I need home, you are that. When I need help, you send yourself. You send Jesus Christ to sympathize with me.

———

I was lonely for years before I was actually divorced. That was probably a red flag I should not have ignored.

But in the past, I felt like the doing of so much alone was leading up to a purpose. I had my job, and he had his. We had plans. I guess I had hope.

There is a difference now facing loneliness after hope is dashed. The Bible says, "Hope deferred makes the heart sick" (Proverb 13:12a). The goal was not to end up alone. The goal was to have connection, stay connected, and explore a whole other season in our life together.

I think God prepared me for this. I don't mean just through loneliness during my marriage, but I felt a preparedness that I think started from birth. To be alone felt like the essence of me. I was returning to an old conversation, not quite over but beginning again 30 years after it first began.

Some personalities are much more observant of the life going on within them. They see the world differently. This isn't a good or bad thing. It is how God created some of us, and I happen to be one of them. I wasn't necessarily bothered by being alone.

My rethinking loneliness began after being unexpectedly pushed back into a state of aloneness. I could not grasp that I would once again be left alone, and I did not want to be alone. I had done everything I thought was right, yet I felt punished. I felt loneliness like never before in my life.

This was a loneliness that I felt I could not find my way through. I wasn't just alone; I could cope with that. This was loneliness that resembled nightmares of being lost when I was a young child.

A retold story of being lost in a desert. I dreamed of swimming with my eyes closed, and when I opened them, I was in a huge bowl of water with high rocky cliffs all around me. I had nightmares of stepping off a school bus, and every single house was blue and white, and a cat sat on the porch of each one. There was no way to know which home was mine, so I cried.

The loneliness after divorce was the utter disconnect from any other human being. I felt like I didn't belong, and no one was waiting for me to arrive safe and sound. People feel loneliness in different ways, which can explain how someone in a room full of friends can still feel lonely.

I knew that being alone could be great. I had read books, explored hobbies, and gone on many many walks alone, feeling wonderful. I enjoyed my own company. My thoughts didn't scare me, and I didn't mind the silence.

If I knew being alone wasn't a bad thing, I wondered why I couldn't rethink loneliness after divorce. I could look at being alone with a brand new purpose, not dependent on anyone else.

My purposes could be pursuing my growth and new freedom; a time to grieve, rest, pray, and read. A time to ask myself, "What do I really want to do with the rest of my life?" This whole second part of life, I felt ready to embrace being alone. I still felt lonely at times, but overall, it became a blessed season of solitude.

I became more self-aware that there were things I did because that was what we did as a couple. I was doing things out of habit. It felt transformative to realize I could do everything differently now that I was divorced and my children were grown and living on their own. I knew I could also look at this time as the point where I disappear into aging not so gracefully.

One way felt powerful, and one way felt like breaking. I searched for inspiration. I found it in certain friendships with women I respected. I found books, podcasts, and groups of women facing the same sort of things as me. I'll share a few of my favorite books and podcasts, but I hope you search for your own as well:

Read:

You Can Survive Divorce: Hope, Healing and Encouragement for Your Journey by Jen Grice

Living Unbroken: Reclaiming Your Life and Your Heart after Divorce by Tracie Miles

Living Alone and Loving It: A Guide to Relishing the Solo Life by Barbara Feldon

The Breakup Bible: The Smart Woman's Guide to Healing From a Breakup or Divorce by Rachel A. Sussman, LCSW

Listen:

Therapy and Theology https://lysaterkeurst.com/therapy-and-theology/

Self-Brain Surgery with Dr. Lee Warren: drleewarren.substack.com

School of Self-Image Podcast with Tonya Leigh: schoolofselfimage.com/podcast

These are just a few of the things I read and listened to that gave me courage and inspiration. Find a good balance between serious information and light-hearted information. Search for counsel from people you respect or you feel are qualified to give it. Seeking God as the final counsel is what helped me actually put good advice into action.

Divorce is not a sentence to loneliness; it's more like a gateway into another season of life that has the potential to be as transforming as you let it be. One day, while searching for a good book to read, I came across a book called *The Way Of The Heart* by Henri Nouwen[8]. In the beginning of this book, he says, "Solitude is the furnace in which this transformation takes [place]." It can be exciting to think about life ahead. It's okay to hope and dream your own new dreams.

A Step Towards Life:

Consider embracing being alone for the purpose of personal growth. A season of being solo will promote a new relationship with yourself. A season of solitude could open up a whole deeper relationship with God if you seek Him.

---

8 Nouwen, Henri J. M. *The Way of the Heart: Desert Spirituality and Contemporary Ministry.* Seabury Press, 1981.

Transforming Loneliness
Into Purposeful Solitude

"But he would withdraw to desolate places and pray."

Luke 5:16

A Note From My Journal: I am not ready to love again. I am not ready to worship. Letting go of one thing before grasping another thing reminds me of a fast before feasting and silence before singing. I need a rest, a retreat before I can worship again.

I recognize my loneliness, and I know I could use someone to keep the feeling away. But I would be using them, and that is unkind…to pretend to love someone, to lie. I can't do that, so I have to face the loneliness and stop it in its tracks.

———

Trust me when I say this: it is better to feel loneliness than to be with the wrong person or even the right person for the wrong reason or wrong time. I believe God is in our circumstances, and everything happens for a reason, like being single after divorce. The temptation after a divorce can be starting a new relationship fueled by my own sense of rejection or my own need to feel cared for or loved.

I also know loneliness makes us feel unwanted and isolated from any hope of love. You might wonder, why not seek people out to make you feel wanted and needed? Someone to fill the unwanted void that the lack of another person's presence brings about. What would a momentary relationship between two adults hurt?

First, we have to remember that the truth is much deeper down. It is the way truth is, most of the time, buried beneath the glaringly obvious. It makes sense that if you are lonely because of your new single status, the answer would be to get into a new relationship as quickly as possible. The problem is that no one person will ever fill the loneliness void, which is why people can be desperately lonely, even in crowds of people or in really great relationships.

Loneliness after divorce or anything traumatic is probably an indication that God is trying to pull you closer to Him. It's delusional to think another person at this time could possibly fill the void that is hurting deep within you. There is a time for relationships and the love of other people, but there is also a time when your Father God longs to comfort, love, and protect you.

I read Henri Nouwen's book, *Reaching Out- The Three Movements of the Spiritual Life*.[9] In the book the first spiritual movement is about reaching out to our innermost selves. He writes this about turning our loneliness into solitude:

> Instead of running away from our loneliness and trying to forget or deny it, we have to protect it and turn it into a fruitful solitude. To live a spiritual life we must first find the courage to enter into the desert of our loneliness and to change it by gentle and persistent efforts into a garden of solitude. This requires not only courage but also a strong faith. As hard as it is to believe that the dry desolate desert can yield endless varieties of flowers, it is equally hard to imagine that our loneliness is hiding unknown beauty. The movement from loneliness to solitude, however, is the beginning of any spiritual life because it is a movement from the restless senses to the restful spirit, from the outward-reaching

---

9 Nouwen, Henri J. M. *Reaching Out: The Three Movements of the Spiritual Life*. Doubleday, 1975.

cravings to the inward-reaching search, from the fearful clinging to the fearless play.

I took my loneliness, and I poured it out to Jesus Christ in prayers, so honest they shocked me. But I knew He already knew my heart, so why not be honest? Tears came easily probably for the first time in my life. These times of prayers and tears left me feeling peaceful enough to where I could sleep.

During this time, the first year of being separated, a friend gave me some advice. She suggested committing a year to being single and just working on myself. I knew I needed this. I questioned so many things in my life. I had to ask myself why I did certain things. In asking this, I realized how important my why was.

I can't say this season of solitude was always enjoyable because it wasn't. Bringing the intellect and emotions into a meeting where both were mutually heard and considered brought up decisions that needed to be made. Truly, it felt like, at times, both had to submit to each other. Some days, it was my mind submitting to emotion, and other days, my emotions submitted to my mind.

I don't think I've ever prayed as openly and honestly as I did throughout this time. I wrote a lot, journaling and blogging. I self-published my first book. I could say I was turning loneliness into a garden of fruitful solitude.

I still felt lonely at times, but I learned so much about myself and about God. It became a haven of rest and peace. There was nobody else to answer to or consider in my plans. I found out I could take care of and handle so many difficult situations.

I had to experience the anxious emotions and give them to God, but asking God for help and forgiveness when I failed was another whole lesson in faith. I'm now in year three of living alone, and

I honestly feel if someone else wanted to be in my life, they would be competing against this life of peace and joy that I am building through Christ, who has strengthened me.

Here are a few suggestions to help you transition your own loneliness into a beautiful and fruitful solitude:

+ Take up courage and face the discomfort of loneliness. This might look like pausing for a moment and admitting to yourself, "I feel lonely." Do what Jesus did while He was here on Earth: find a solitary and quiet place. Look at this as an invitation to unburden your heart and mind by praying honestly and openly to God.

+ Stay aware. Ask yourself why you are doing whatever it is you are doing. Stretch, walk, or just sit in silence as you consider your own thoughts and contemplate your own emotions. Try to identify your "why." What is your motivation behind doing, feeling, or thinking the way you do? Once you have identified your motivation, do a search in God's Word to see what He has to say about it.

+ Be gentle but persistent. Think about what is true. Even when your mind wanders, bring it back gently and persistently to the truth you are trying to hold onto. What words keep coming up?

+ Meditate on God's Word. Find a verse that resonates with you and your situation that day and go over it multiple times a day.

+ Imagine the possible ways you could bring beauty, growth, exploration, fun, and joy into your life. Have your own back during this time. Don't be dismissive to your own soul.. Ask yourself, "What do you really want and really need, and how can you get that independently of anyone else?"

+ The goal of solitude is experiencing solace and providence from God, not other people. Learn where and how you best sense the presence of God. Set aside time every day to meet with Him there. This could be walking beside a lake or sitting silently with a candle lit, waiting on words to come.

A Step Towards Life:

Consider reading the books, *Reaching Out or The Way of the Heart*[10] by Henri Nouwen. Both books convinced me it was worth the effort to take my loneliness and exchange it for a time of solitude. Answering the invitation from God to step away from everyone else and spend time with Him healing our brokenness.

---

10 Nouwen, Henri J. M. *The Way of the Heart: Connecting with God Through Prayer, Wisdom, and Silence.* HarperOne, 1981.

On Delight in God and
Our Desires

"Delight yourself in the LORD,
and he will give you the desires of your heart."

Psalm 37:4

A Note From My Journal: He asked me once why I cared about feminism since it's never really touched my life. It's so sad he truly knew me so little, or he did know me but chose to disregard how I had been affected. . The more time that goes by with me on the outside now looking in at this marriage I see us both so much clearer. In spite of his love for me, respect for me as a human being with my own ambitions and desires was sadly lacking. I wish I had been bolder and more confident in the knowledge that God loved me.

Growing up in church, it seemed as if getting married and having children was the ultimate goal of a Christian woman. Yet the world around me at the time showed me women doing many things besides just getting married and raising children. I knew I wanted to be one of these women. I am grateful for the women that gave me hope, that I, too, could go to college, work, and create an income of my own.

The ultimate goal for any woman is wherever the God-given desires of her heart have guided her to be. No person, man or woman, can tell you who you are or what you are meant for in this world.

There is no favoritism with God. He loves us each individually and is perfecting each of us in his own time according to his will. We know life has many seasons and different landscapes in each one. We won't be able to remain in any season forever or rush through any one season, no matter how much we try.

The best thing we can do is decide to delight in the ways we get to discover God anew in each season of life. To delight is to be captivated by the everyday workings of another. The same way we watch our children learn to walk and speak and ultimately create their own lives out in the world. The joy and gratification of seeing a person, place, or thing come into their own full being is what delight really is.

We have our own personalities, will, quirks, and fears. God already knows each of these things about us. As we grow up, we try different things and begin to realize what we like and what we don't like. Sometimes, other people convince us fear is needed, anxiety is the way, and life is easier if we just delight in the same things, but all along the way, God is our Maker and offers something that looks a lot more like his image and his kingdom.

God delights in seeing us come to our own full potential just as much as we delight in seeing Him arrive in our lives in all the ways we hoped and prayed He would. We don't get to see God fully on this earthly side of eternity. But whatever season or landscape we are experiencing, He makes promises for those who love and obey Him right here and right now:

- "The thief comes only to steal and kill and destroy. I came that they may have life and have it abundantly." John 10:10
- "...but the Lord takes pleasure in those who fear him, in those who hope in his steadfast love." Psalm 147:11
- "Or which one of you, if his son asks him for bread, will give him a stone? Or if he asks for a fish, will give him

a serpent? If you then, who are evil, know how to give good gifts to your children, how much more will your Father who is in heaven give good things to those who ask him!" Matthew 7:9-11

As we watch God respond to us through his words, the actions of others, and our circumstances, our faith grows. Confidence in Christ comes a little easier each time his providence is noticed. He created us for an abundant life and fellowship with Him. We see the abundant life right in the middle of our tears and difficulties.

It is in the difficulties that we are the most blessed as we navigate through every landscape and every season meant for us. He knows the desires we have to get through the grief of divorce and not just barely make it but to come out even better on the other side of this divorce. Be captivated as you watch what God does. With every heartfelt prayer, you reveal yourself more to Him. Not that He didn't already know you, but your prayers and honesty invite Him the same way He first invited you to His love.

A Step Towards Life:

How can you delight in God? Is there an area of life that God is showing you a little more of Himself? It may be just noticing something small like the perfect timing of words. It could be a prayer answered after months of pouring your heart out to God. Noticing God is delight. Saying thank you and allowing your soul to reflect on God's goodness is a form of worship we can experience in our everyday lives.

Life or Death

"For this commandment that I command you today is not too hard for you, neither is it far off. It is not in heaven, that you should say, 'Who will ascend to heaven for us and bring it to us, that we may hear it and do it?' Neither is it beyond the sea, that you should say, 'Who will go over the sea for us and bring it to us, that we may hear it and do it?' But the word is very near you. It is in your mouth and in your heart so that you can do it.

See, I have set before you today life and good, death and evil…"

Deuteronomy 30:11-15

A Note From My Journal: It's going to be hard, lonely, and difficult no matter what I choose, whether I accept my plight or fight it. Someone said your ability to adapt is your ability to survive. This is so true. One way of struggling brings new life, and another way of struggling causes me to die. The life set before me right now is loving God with all my heart and soul through every little thing.

Marriage is something we are taught to work hard for and work hard to keep. In a healthy, faithful, and loving marriage, we have no problem working together to find ways to live and love each other peacefully. It's a desirable work to face difficulties together and find our way through as a couple. But many marriages end because the other partner has decided they don't want to take part in a marriage anymore. A toxic or abusive relationship has emerged, and we have to answer for ourselves whether we choose life or death for ourselves.

Marriage is a blessing not to be taken lightly. Being single is a blessing to be cherished and not looked down upon as less than. I want to work hard now at being single and feeling happy and be just as fulfilled as a married woman, maybe even more so. There has been a stigma associated with singlehood, as if you are to be pitied because you are alone, as if you are only half of something bigger and better.

The truth is there are more single women, especially in the 50 and above age frame, than ever before. What would it look like if we decided to work hard on being single by exploring singlehood as a choice, not because you lack anything but because you enjoy yourself and you are ready to create the life you truly desire? There is great freedom in being single if we choose to do the following:

+ Actively take steps to be more aligned with your personal goals and values. Our beliefs and actions should align. This is integrity.

+ Learn more about God through praying and then doing or not doing what God has revealed. We must walk out the truth God shows us in every aspect of life.

+ Shift focus away from an ex and onto ourselves. You are the only one you can change. Focus on your own development. This keeps us humble and keeps us from judging what is no longer any of our business.

+ Many of us lose ourselves in a marriage. We are distracted and do get wrapped up in our spouses wants and needs. This isn't necessarily a bad thing within a loving marriage, but we are no longer married so it is time to shift the focus.

+ Choose practical things for ourselves like meals to eat, where to live, where to travel, how your home is arranged, and how you celebrate holidays. These can be fun things to explore and change as you get more in touch with your own soul.

+ Set boundaries around what is and is not allowed in your life. You get to choose life and then build upon with wisdom and understanding. Protect your new life with boundaries for others as well as for yourself.

We may find ourselves alone, but we are not doomed in any way. There is so much hope in what the future holds patiently for us. Our joy is as close as one honest thought realized or one lying, destroying thought taken captive. If we suffer, why not let it be for what we really want even if it's hard?

When you think about daily ways of living your life, ask yourself: Is this bringing me closer to what feels like life to my soul? We all obey the principles of someone or something. Why not let it be God and his goodness? Obedience to God leads to life.

I know this is a hard truth for some people, and the word obey has all kinds of misguided negative connotations in the world today. As Christians, we see God differently because we know Him in an intimate way that others who do not believe in Him are unable to understand. We have felt his guidance and experienced his love through joy and grief.

A Christian experiences God as much or as little as we allow. If we ignore God in our life, then we will remain spiritually immature, still a Christian but not living the close relational life that you are invited to. You settle for a life less abundant in all the deep and meaningful things.

Eugene Peterson explains in his book, *A Long Obedience in the Same Direction*[11]:

> "There is a great market for religious experience in our world; there is little enthusiasm for the patient acquisition of virtue, little inclination to sign up for a long apprenticeship in what earlier generations of Christians called holiness."

Imagine God saying to you, "See, I have set before you today life and good, death and evil" (Deuteronomy 30:11-15). Choosing life looks like love toward God, yourself, and others. We get to grow more Christ-like every time we say yes to obedience and the life God has given us.

Choosing life also looks like treating yourself with gentleness, kindness, and nurturing. Don't say unkind things about yourself because your brain will eventually believe what you tell it repeatedly. Treat yourself as you would treat someone else with compassion and empathy.

Something that helped me be gentler with myself when the pain of divorce caused my mind to think the worst about myself was looking at a photo of myself as a four-year-old. I was standing with my aunt and my brother. I remember looking at that picture and seeing a sweet, shy girl who had the same expression on her face that my daughter used to have at the same age. I was still that girl. I wanted to protect her, hold her hand, and encourage her forward.

---

11 Peterson, Eugene H. *A Long Obedience in the Same Direction: Discipleship in an Instant Society.* InterVarsity Press, 1980.

A Step Towards Life:

Consider the paths set before you right now. Which one seems more obedient to the person God is guiding you to be? Journal your own list of choices that represent life or death.

A New Routine

"All things are lawful," but not all things are helpful. "All things are lawful," but not all things build up."

1 Corinthians 10:22-23

A Note From My Journal: I am trying to keep myself happy moment by moment. But evening comes, and I remember the meals I used to cook when the children were home. When he still loved me. I can't deny the comfort of ice cream when thoughts of dinner make me sad.

I remember the first months of living alone. I could work all day and be fine until dinner time. Deciding what was for dinner could bring on a surge of despair for me. Cooking for one person didn't seem worth the effort. Sometimes, I'd eat ice cream or popcorn or just have a glass of wine, all of which only exasperated the sadness.

My first decision about a new evening ritual set around dinner may seem like a small thing, but it was truly transforming. I started ordering a meal subscription box. I told myself it was just to get me started on eating a healthy dinner. It did seem like a small luxury, but I soon realized it wasn't all that expensive for one person.

There was little waste because all the ingredients were measured out. I didn't have to buy a five-pound bag of potatoes or a pound of meat and eat leftovers all week. It was fun to pick out my meals online, and I started looking forward to cooking for myself with all the right ingredients delivered right to my door.

I found it grounded me by giving me something to look forward to in the evening. Ice cream still tempted me, but I was at least making a small change in my routine that definitely began to make me feel and think better. Cooking was something I needlessly was tasking myself with, and it only brought on sadness. There was no reason to cook a meal like I used to, and there was nothing wrong with allowing myself to cook easier meals that actually felt comforting just for me.

I cannot deny the difference between how I feel after a nourishing meal and how I feel after something much less nourishing. If you notice some routine that brings on sadness or unwanted memories, get creative and find a way to change it around or eliminate it completely. Be patient and kind with yourself. Eating and drinking the wrong things isn't the end of the world, but it can produce negative consequences if left unchecked.

Remember, there are many things that might be lawful, but it isn't necessarily helpful if it leads to overindulgence or we use it as a coping mechanism. A lot of the time, choosing one way over another is realizing what is most helpful for our body, mind, and soul at any particular time. It wasn't a sin to cook when I didn't feel like it, nor was it a sin to order a subscription food service that gave me a break. Like everything else that God gives us that is meant for good, we, as creative human beings, can find ways to overuse, underuse, idolize, or pervert it.

Instead, be mindful of God's gifts and use them with thanksgiving towards Him. It's impossible to honestly thank God for a gift and then use it to destroy the good for which it was meant. This is actually mocking God.

We don't have to be a slave to anything. God gives us so much liberty. Life has shifted, and we need to adjust. There are healthy alternative routines that might fit us better in this season of life.

Here are a few ideas to switch one way of being into an alternative way of being. These are based on common feelings that are experienced during the grief caused by divorce. These emotions are allowed. Just remember these emotions should be questioned before they are acted upon. These ideas are to build you up and help you focus on the liberty you have to actually do the most beneficial thing.

Anger: For anger during the divorce process in particular, there will be times when you will have to be confrontational. I know this boldness can be uncomfortable for some people, it was for me. Feel free to step away for a short time to gather your thoughts and the right words to articulate your feelings about the situation. When you are ready to confront the person and the problem, do so honestly, even if it's uncomfortable.

There will be other times that no confrontation will be needed, but it would be helpful to journal about the situation or talk to a trusted friend. The most important thing is to make sure you don't suppress it or just let it go. The reality is we don't let things go. Anger gets pushed down inside us, and resentment and rehearsing the wrong done to us will paralyze us.

Depressed: Talk with a friend, a life coach, or a therapist once a week. Someone who allows you to speak freely and openly. Someone who asks the right questions that aid in shifting your perspective. Read and learn about neuroplasticity- the ability of the brain to form and reorganize synaptic connections, especially in response to learning or experience or following injury. We can change our own brains! Our thoughts and our habits can change from pessimism to hope.

Overwhelm: Drop something as no longer important enough to take up your time and energy. Replace it with something that is much more helpful, like my ordering a meal subscription box and eliminating meal prep and grocery shopping. What could you eliminate and/or add?

Restlessness: Go for a long hike in nature. Or a short run in a park. Take a fitness class. Do a streaming online class. Take a bike ride at sunset or an early morning brisk walk and watch the sunrise.

Exhaustion: End your day early. Take a hot bubble bath and have a comforting meal in bed on a tray. Read a fiction book or watch a movie. Sleep. Spend a Saturday or Sunday napping, reading, journaling. Practice some silence and solitude to rest your brain and your emotions.

These are a few things that could be turned into a weekly or monthly routine. Pick and choose, experiment, and see what actually helps you.

A Step Towards Life:

Create a new routine or ritual. Implement one new routine or ritual each month. At the end of the month, decide if it is working for you or against you. Keep it or get rid of it, or try again the next month. Take your time and be patient with yourself if it's a difficult new routine.

Walking Back into the World as Just You

"Whoever isolates himself seeks his own desire; he breaks out against all sound judgment."

Proverbs 18:1

A Note From My Journal: Of course, I want to go, but I don't want to walk into a new church in a new town, newly separated and single, and feeling strange about going back to church as a divorced woman. There is comfort in knowing God understands. I will be blessed if I can just walk in.

———

It sounds like a small thing: going to church alone for the first time as a woman divorced. It's not exactly that I didn't want to go, but more like I wanted the feeling of comfort that comes after doing the uncomfortable thing. I was a little fearful, and I anticipated the awkwardness if anyone asked if I was married. I knew I could stay home, but deep down, I knew my soul was lonely, and it would be such a blessing to be among other Christians again.

I felt the Holy Spirit strongly this morning. I knew if I stayed home, I would be settling for much less than what I really wanted. I knew God would bless me like He has before when I've known the right thing to do and have done it. On a Sunday in December, I was fighting an inner battle. I took a few deep, calming breaths and walked into a new church in a new town.

Just Jennifer. That's all I felt. I had the inner dialogue of the Holy Spirit helping me; it had been there all morning.

A young woman greeted me, and I told her that this was my first time there. She offered up the couples' Sunday school class but then quickly told me there was also a women's class. I was feeling relieved as she directed me to a class of all women. Everyone was nice, and there was even another divorced woman in the class, who shared before ever knowing my story.

The class was studying Because of Bethlehem by Max Lucado. This Sunday morning, we were discussing preparing space for Christ, making room in our hearts right now. I felt deeply ready for Advent like never before. I was ready for this Christmas to be bent toward making room in my heart and my mind for Jesus to abide.

I had never really considered myself as an inn or a manger the way this study taught it, and the ladies in the class discussed it. " How do I make room?" " How did I make space for God today?" My favorite question that morning was, "How can I allow God to love me in this moment?" Advent hit me on a soul-stirring level.

I was exactly where I needed to be. Honoring Sabbath in this new place. Making room in my emptied-out life for connection to the kind women in front of me. As the weeks went by and we continued in the study, I came no closer to being excited about Christmas as a holiday, but Advent, for this, I felt a longing to celebrate.

I was too sad this first Christmas season without my family being together to feel joy the way I used to. God worked this out, I think, by shifting my perspective to the deep spiritual truth that is the essence of this season we celebrate Jesus Christ. I had hardly recognized it was the Christmas season earlier that morning as I had struggled to get myself to church.

I felt such kindness from these women. My heart was full of thanksgiving for the way the Holy Spirit strengthened me to move through awkward feelings and for showing me the blessedness of obeying out of trust. A trust birthed from God's unwavering and relentless love that never fails me.

I hope you are beginning to walk back out into the world. We can't stay isolated or hidden away and still relish the abandonment of our soul to God. Connection with others lets us know we are not alone. Other people give light to dark places within us that we cannot see. We are light, and we are salt, just like Jesus said.

A Step Towards Life:

It might be time to walk back into the world. Hopefully, you have had plenty of solitude and rest, that has helped you heal. You may be changed in many ways. You will never be exactly the same without the person you are leaving behind. Yet, there is a kind of excitement in realizing you have not yet met all the people or done all the things that are meant for you in the upcoming years, months, and days.

Name a step you can take to get out into a like-minded group. You might go back to church, join a class, or travel and just be around people.

When Nature Points Us to God's Faithfulness

"The steadfast love of the LORD never ceases;
his mercies never come to an end;
they are new every morning;
great is your faithfulness."

Lamentations 3:22-23

Note From my Journal: When I step away from all the differing opinions of what should or should not be done, I walk outside into the woods again. The promise God gave me was to be able to rest once again right here and right now. How is walking rest? That in itself seems divinely inspired. I find in the silence, it is easier to disregard the overflow of too much information. I just need to see geese flying triangular in the winter sky.

The hymn "Great Is Thy Faithfulness" drifts in and out of my mind. I see the geese overhead, and I remember a few years back when I walked outside in February a large, lone goose sat on the ground. I was afraid to approach it, so I watched it. Then, I went inside and looked up, "Why would one goose be sitting alone in the winter?"

There were a few differing opinions of why a goose would be sitting alone. It could have lost its mate and be mourning. It could be that they aren't alone but are sitting while their mate is nearby on an egg. A lone goose could also be injured and waiting for another flock to join.

Whatever the reason it had for stopping in the first place, something about this goose alone and waiting to get back on the right path seemed meaningful to me. At that time, I had recently decided to take my writing seriously and joined a writers group. I had started and stopped writing throughout the years while working part-time at other jobs. I had been feeling restless and unsure about this new step towards writing.

The goose was a sort of sign for me. Watching this flock of geese above me today, I remember that lone goose, and I recollect the words that taught me about the reason why the goose was alone in the first place. The hope that it would be returning to the right path soon. In the same way, I would find my path. It was a reassurance that all of creation sometimes derails from the original plans.

I will stop and rest. I can wait for new life to be safely born into existence. I will cling to the wisdom of how much better it is to wait for the people who welcome me into their lives than settle for scraps from people that can take me or leave me. When I am unfaithful, by going to everyone but God, He remains faithful. I can pretend I'm busy and that I didn't know that God feels jealousy, anger, and hurt the same way I do.

God's faithfulness demands a response from us. A response that, in essence, claims we see Him. Do we hear Him, and are we so expectant of his movement in our lives that nothing is an accidental occurrence? I saw His movement that February day when the goose sat in my yard the same way I heard His words return again years later as geese flew over my head.

I will once again be on the right path, even after everything this divorce has done to me. It can be the same with you. You may recognize God's faithfulness in different ways than me. I often sense God in nature; this is how God gets my attention.

How do you sense God's faithfulness towards you? It's a personal experience between you and the Holy Spirit within you. Maybe you aren't sure, but now that it's been brought to your attention, perhaps you can begin noticing God's faithfulness every day. Because He is faithful and shows us mercies each and every day.

A Step Towards Life:

The Holy Spirit helps us recognize God's words and movement in our lives. The Spirit also speaks to God the unsaid words written on our hearts. Note God's faithfulness as the Spirit helps you remember and say a prayer of thanksgiving. Live an observant life that responds back faithfully.

Letting Go

"Keep your life free from love of money, and be content
with what you have, for he has said, 'I will never leave you
nor forsake you.' So we can confidently say,

'The Lord is my helper;
I will not fear;
what can man do to me?'"

Hebrews 13:5-6

*A Note From My Journal: I can love things without possessing them.
I can admire. I can enjoy. I can be content not owning things. I can be
thankful for what I have and what I've had, but I don't need it anymore.*

*Why do any of us hold onto things? Old journals, old clothes, books
that impacted me twenty years ago, that big huge pot I used to make chili
and soup in. I think it's a feeling of fear for me. If I give things up, I fear
that part of my life will be forgotten.*

*Thirty years of paraphernalia is suffocating me. I know this house-
ful of stuff and boxes brimming with some things I thought I wanted and
some things I took to make him mad, but of course, it didn't because he
didn't care. Maybe that's another reason I'm holding on: to understand,
to look at all the pieces, and to look for clues. But God has moved me right
here. This is my present, and I am invited to trust Him on this journey
of getting rid of what no longer serves me. God never changes, but He
changes us. Let me not look back like Lot's wife turning into salt. Forever
a preservative paralyzed and unmovable.*

When I first moved out of the home I shared with my husband and into my new house, I had no understanding how drastically different my life would be. I brought too much furniture, home decor, pots and pans, and Christmas ornaments. It was too much. It was too much for a single divorced woman with grown children.

One day, as I was surrounded by boxes and furniture, I broke down and cried. Memories of the years of being a military family and moving with excited anticipation mocked me. In the past, I could get a houseful of boxes unpacked, a new home set up, and get the kids enrolled in school in a matter of weeks. Now, six months later, with boxes and clutter everywhere, I was beginning to see my problem.

I had an eye-opening realization that not only did I not need so much stuff, but it made me sad to even look at some of it. My heart was in scarcity mode, so it didn't seem logical to sell some of these things. I was living in fear. I was allowing fear to literally close me into a space in which I had no desire to be.

It made me wonder what I would actually take with me if I could keep only a few necessary things. I made a list that afternoon. How drastically different my list of valuable things looked like compared to the overwhelming view before me.

My list had things on it that highlighted a sparser life that encouraged my writing life. Things like my desk, shelves, and laptop. My Kindle Scribe and some of my books were at the top of my list. Some framed art had to go because it just did not fit what I wanted on my walls anymore. A lot did not make my list, and it still felt difficult to let go.

In my head, I heard familiar and rational questions like, "What if I need it later or my kids want it?" Keeping things we don't really need in the present season of life feels like misguided hope instead of actual hope. Actual hope is for growing and prospering forward and not remaining in the claustrophobic past.

I was free once I decided I needed to get rid of a lot of stuff. I felt clearer and calmer as I sold, donated, and threw away things. I found more space for the things I needed in this new season of life. Some sentimental things, like old journals and artwork my children had made, were difficult to throw away. I picked my favorites and left the rest behind.

I applied the advice from the famous textile maker William Morris to not hold onto things that were not useful or beautiful to me. I picked the useful things that I could picture my future self minus a husband and children using. I picked the best objects and gifts given that portrayed the beauty of the person who gave it. I had a feeling of guilt boxing up two blue and white mugs my daughter had gifted me, but I knew deep down she still loved me and would never be hurt over me changing my kitchen to fresh new colors.

Months later, I showed my daughter the new dishes, and she said she liked them better, but she would miss the blue and white. In the end, these things that fill up our homes are simply things and have no real power. You are the one who gives power to these things.

A Step Towards Life:

What are you holding onto out of fear or guilt? Fear can be tricky at times because you might not even recognize it. Fear of needing an object or the guilt of hurting someone's feelings can cause us to hold on too tight and much too long. Think about your future self, new dreams, and new goals. Make your own list of the most essential things you would pack up if you had to leave immediately.

This can be eye-opening as you disengage with the past and only have a cloudy vision of the future. What needs to be removed or given away? What causes you to smile and what makes you sad? The answers are your clues to hold it or let it go.

Living with Intention

"So teach us to number our days
that we may get a heart of wisdom."

Psalm 90:12

A Note From My Journal: There are practical things I know. I need an income, a house to live in, and food to eat. Maybe I can have a simple and calm life. A home of my own and not having to move again would bring me stability. A work I enjoyed but challenged me daily would give me direction. Money with no ties to anyone but myself would be freeing. I need a church to fellowship with others who share a love for the same God as me. For the first time in my life, I can make course corrections without considering anyone else. I guess I could have before, but I never did, and maybe that is exactly why I am where I am right now.

I am realizing how much of my true self and desires I neglected and rationalized as not really that important. But this was so wrong! There is a life to live differently now. A new life where my very lifestyle keeps me spiritually fit is what I envision and hope for. I know my soul needs care, and the Holy Spirit needs to be acknowledged.

What kind of a woman do you desire to be? In Jean Fleming's book, *Pursue The Intentional Life*,[12] she keeps track of what she calls her Old Woman File. At first, it was just a note she scribbled down while taking a walk when she turned fifty.

---

12 Fleming, Jean. *Pursue the Intentional Life*. NavPress, 2013.

She prayed about the kind of older woman she would become at this halfway point in her life. She desired to be intentional and focused, not tossed about aimlessly, never considering where she was going or what she was doing. What began as a note on a walk became the book she wrote from her collected verses, quotes, insights, and anything else relevant to a woman desiring to live intentionally in the second half of life.

This book challenged me in such an exciting way. I started my own "Aging Gracefully File." I used Pinterest for inspiring images. I read about this mid-life season, and some of my aspirations came from women I encountered who made me curious about being a strong woman of God until the very end of my life. Their habits inspired me, so I decided on a few concrete things that I desired for my future.

One decision was I wanted to be the kind of older woman who went to church even if she was alone. I don't think the woman who inspired this thought ever knew that seeing her step out of her truck in front of a church with stained glass windows on a busy city street would spark an intention within me. An aspiration to be this kind of woman led me to go to church alone. I desired to be what I thought her to be. The kind of woman who still dresses up and goes to church, even when everyone would understand if she stayed home.

It was Sunday morning, and it was snowing when I saw this lady get out of her truck and walk into church. I remember thinking she could probably stay home safe and warm, and everyone would understand. It was this scene that filed itself away in my brain that later reemerged and gave me the courage I needed to not only go to church alone but anywhere else I had a desire to go but had felt reluctant to go because I was alone.

It's interesting how God gives us these scenes in life. They seem so ordinary and basic until we really observe all the details of God's well-lit and perfectly-timed curriculum. It is these moments when we become inspired to be like someone or something that clue us in on what we might decide will be part of our own intentional life. I've often wondered why I've seen certain things, but it always seems to come full circle eventually. It's an important note to make as we think about our future selves and make our own intentions.

Nothing is accidental, and every scene in our life happens for a reason. God is using our entire life for his love to be illuminated. When you gather up all of your life this far, consider the recurring themes. What are the true God-given desires of your heart?

What sort of characteristics do you aspire to? Our values, our intentions, and aspirations are personal to each of us. After all, Jesus is a personal Savior who invites us to friendship with Him. Notice the things you don't do and ask yourself why. Your reason why you do something or don't do something can work like a scale weighing out our deeper motivations. Sometimes, we don't do something because we are simply too afraid to do it, not because we honestly don't want to do it.

My own "old woman file" that I renamed for myself, "Aging Gracefully File" would include wisdom on a life I could delight in and not be ashamed of at the end of my life. I see a life built on faithful and intentional ground. I would follow in the footsteps of Jean Flemings as she says,

"God is not asking me to number my days to increase my pace but rather to examine my route, not to increase my efficiency but to see where I must make course corrections in heart, character, and actions."

We are blessed with time, and hopefully, we redeem it to our own intentional life even when it might be more convenient to stay comfortable and safe. The world is more than happy to steal our time, eating it up and leaving us with regrets and excuses for not doing the good things that God has planned for us. In Ephesians, we are warned to be wise with our time,

> "Look carefully then how you walk, not as unwise but as wise, making the best use of the time, because the days are evil. Therefore do not be foolish, but understand what the will of the Lord is" (Ephesians 5:15-17).

A Step Towards Life:

Create your own old woman file. Name it whatever you want. Fill it up with your own intentions and aspirations.

God's Unchanging Love

"Jesus Christ is the same yesterday and today and forever."

Hebrews 13:8

A Note From My Journal: Lord, You lift me out of miry clay and the horrible pit. I prayed for Your help, and I see clearly how you rescued me. I stand with knowledge on a firm foundation that doesn't give way. But I cannot take even one step.

I know in the deep recesses of my mind that as much as others love me and I love them, ultimately, they are not God, and neither am I. Love can change. People will and should change. But God never changes.

"God is not human, that he should lie,
not a human being, that he should change his mind.

Does he speak and then not act?
Does he promise and not fulfill?"

Numbers 23:19, NIV

God does not lie. His love never leaves me. His love has been since the beginning when He deemed Creation good, and then He proclaimed human life as very good. He doesn't change His mind about loving us and being merciful to us.

This can be hard to grasp with our human minds because it seems so unnatural to continue to love even when rejected or treated badly. But isn't it good news that God still loves us and feels mercy towards us even when we disappoint Him, deny Him, and treat Him unkindly by our careless actions and words? It is like a double-edged sword, though, isn't it? When it comes to other people that we feel deserve punishment instead of love or mercy, we seem to hope God has a bit of a higher standard for justice than He did for us.

God is unchanging and unwavering in being Himself. A.W. Tozer writes, "To say God is immutable is to say that He never differs from Himself. The concept of a growing or developing God is not found in Scriptures."[13]

I know it is me who changes, not my God. He is already holy while I am still being perfected. I desire to grow towards God, not further away. We each decide this for ourselves. It is our will that needs developing, which happens every time we either set our mind to obey or to disobey. It is us that needs to grow and to mature, not God.

I find myself stuck, unable to take the next step. This is after I've already experienced God lifting me to safety. It is as if the miry clay still clings to me, weighing me down, and I cannot take a step in any direction. Is this being paralyzed with fear?

We want consistency and stability along with a clear view of the path ahead. God gives us Himself, not a clear path. The consistency He gives us is knowing if we get lost again, He will find us and once again place us on stable ground (Numbers 23:19). I'm realizing I have to walk encumbered with difficulties at times, but being encumbered is not being paralyzed.

It is just a trial, and we already know experiencing trials is a state of blessedness. The blessedness is in the constant way He walks with us. The comfort and peace in knowing there is no wrong di-

---

13 Tozer, A. W. *The Knowledge of the Holy: The Attributes of God: Their Meaning in the Christian Life.* Harper & Row, 1961.

rection sometimes. God just wants us to take a step. A faith-filled movement in any direction because we believe with all our heart and soul that our God remains unchanging and his love unwavering.

Going through divorce has been the hardest thing I've ever gone through. It has been three years since my ex-husband told me he wanted to get divorced. I have changed in so many ways during this time. I have found God in every step of the way. Even when I had weeks or months where fear stopped me, God always caused me to eventually look at Him directly once again. His promise remained the same, "I will instruct you and teach you in the way you should go; I will counsel you with my eye upon you" (Psalm 32:8).

There were many times I prayed because I had absolutely no idea what to do next. I found answers; some answers were put right in front of me, and others I had to search diligently for. But there were always answers. I thought I'd never make it through to any kind of happiness and you might be feeling that way too.

Rest in knowing your prayers are heard, and your tears are always noticed by the God who loves you. You will get through. God will get you through, and you will be changed by grief. You will also be changed by the love God pours out on you.

A Step Towards Life:

Meditate on or write in your journal the ways you have experienced God's attribute of being unchanging or immutable. Our circumstances are different, and God is creative in his ways of reaching each of us. Thankfully, He remembers each of us and knows our every circumstance. In his dealings with his people there is a beautiful creativity that is always expressing the same unchanging love.

Finding Home

"By wisdom a house is built,
and by understanding it is established;
by knowledge the rooms are filled
with all precious and pleasant riches."

Proverbs 24:3

A Note From My Journal: We are building this house. You and I slowly and steadily, through wisdom and understanding, build. How greatly my view of home has changed. Once it was a destination, a place to finally be, I still want that. A built home to live within, but there is a deeper and different home that looks like a soul at peace during the storms; it looks like Jesus sleeping during the storm at sea.

———

Home has always seemed elusive to me. Yet I remember being so young and praying for a home of my own. I imagined every small thing. I hoped for woods that would surround us and the big fluffy towels we would have. I don't remember everything I prayed about my future home, but the point is I was young and praying for a home. Now I'm 51 and still praying for a home.

Probably, being married to a Marine didn't help. Moving every few years didn't help me feel settled, although I enjoyed everywhere we lived, and it was all an adventure that I'm happy I got to experience. These circumstances were at times exciting and fun but other times unbearably lonely, friendless, jobless, and purposeless. I experienced these things off and on throughout the years, but they weren't mine for more than four or five years at a time. It's hard to feel at home when you know it will be gone soon.

In the past, I could unpack boxes quickly and set up our home in a matter of days, so why was it taking me almost three years to unpack and create my home now after divorce? A few reasons come to mind, such as grief being at the top of the list. I look back with regret at my willingness to leave my home even though it was my ex that had been unfaithful. But my state of mind at that time would not allow me to stay.

I was rash in moving away. The beautiful thing about God in my situation was the way He found me during that late summer walk I took on my land. Seeds were planted. It would take another year of me being unhappy living in the house into which I had so rashly moved.

I found God repeating verses like,

"Unless the LORD builds the house,
those who build it labor in vain." Psalm 127:1a

"The wisest of women builds her house,
but folly with her own hands tears it down." Proverbs 14:1

There were other verses, and they all had the common theme of building. They were about how God builds outward foundations as well as inner structures for our souls. One verse that struck me the most is:

"Do you not know that you are God's temple and that God's Spirit dwells in you? If anyone destroys God's temple, God will destroy him. For God's temple is holy, and you are that temple."

1 Corinthians 3:16-17

The reality was that the place I had moved to was not working for me. I tried to make it work, but the truth was I was settling for so much less than I deeply desired. This desire I knew was from God trying to nourish my soul. I would have to let go of my stubbornness and release my grip because this house as beautiful as it was and the new town as friendly as some people were, none of it was for me. I once again faced the fact that to be healthy mentally, spiritually, and physically I would have to move.

I could not let the fear of moving stop me. For the first time in my life, I was deciding where I wanted to live. I thought about what I really wanted and needed from a place. I took my time and didn't make any rash or hasty decisions this time.

I set a list of priorities that I felt were important for my well-being. By wisdom from God and knowledge of myself I trusted I would find and create a brand new home somewhere, somehow. These verses were a guide to me.

Proverbs 24:3 reminded me to think about the knowledge I already possessed about myself. What I could and could not live with or without to feel at home. By knowledge, rooms would be filled. The knowledge of what God requires of me and the knowledge of what kind of place nourishes me and makes me more capable to be the woman God created me to be.

Psalm 127:1 acted as a scaffolding for me as I searched for houses and explored the idea of building a cabin on my land. I knew I wanted God to direct me to my next home. I didn't want to waste any more time in vain attempts to find my own home. The Lord had to build it. I knew this with all my heart.

Proverbs 14:1 and 1 Corinthians 3:16-17 challenged me to remember who I am as the abiding place of the Holy Spirit. God's temple, God's home needed to be cared for and built up rather than torn down by my own carelessness.

When thinking about our home, whether you move after divorce or you stay in the house you once shared, challenge the notion that you are stuck. Ask yourself what really nourishes your body, mind, and soul. You are not stuck or trapped. You may be like me and be fearful of moving once again or decide your income won't support you. There are a million fearful possibilities. There could be just as many worries in remaining where you are.

Only a truthful examination of your life can reveal where you need to be and where God desires to bless you with his best and not the mediocre or good enough.

A Step Towards Life:

Maybe you feel lost after divorce. It's not just the end of a relationship; it is an end of a way of life. Take your time, but decide where you want to live. Maybe it is the marital home, or maybe you want to start over somewhere else. Give yourself time to get clarity about what you want, not what others tell you is the best idea. You are the one who has to live in a place.

What do you really want? Where do you feel contentment and like God is building? Consider you have inner work to do first. Your thoughts, attitudes, and habits might need to be examined.

The Beauty of Showing Each Other Our Scars

"Now Thomas, one of the twelve, called the Twin, was not with them when Jesus came. So the other disciples told him, "We have seen the Lord." But he said to them, "Unless I see in his hands the mark of the nails, and place my finger into the mark of the nails, and place my hand into his side, I will never believe."

Eight days later, his disciples were inside again, and Thomas was with them. Although the doors were locked, Jesus came and stood among them and said, "Peace be with you." Then he said to Thomas, "Put your finger here, and see my hands; and put out your hand, and place it in my side. Do not disbelieve, but believe." Thomas answered him, "My Lord and my God!" Jesus said to him, "Have you believed because you have seen me? Blessed are those who have not seen and yet have believed."

John 20:24-29

A Note From My Journal: I didn't believe I'd recover from my loss of love. My life was divided, and I felt destroyed. But there were a thousand moments that God gave me comfort. This sounds so trite, so small. That God happened to my life the same way Jesus happened to Thomas's life. Maybe comfort is the wrong word. But there were a thousand moments that God placed my finger on the mark of death, there was a hole in my heart, and there was a hole in my Lord's hand. God felt like flesh and blood beside me. Emmanuel God with us; this is more accurate.

I think I would have been like Thomas. I would need to see pierced flesh where I knew the wounds would be to believe that this same man was Jesus Christ risen from the grave after crucifixion. The most beautiful thing about Jesus appearing to Thomas is the one-on-one attention given to Thomas in the midst of his doubting.

It's so personal, so real to be invited to put your hand on someone else's wound. The visualization of this moment speaks vividly to me of a personal relationship with Christ. It looks shocking yet beautiful. There is no shame in our limited ability to believe or see salvation and healing, at least until we are invited to touch the proof. It doesn't have to be a lot of belief, a small amount will do. Remember the man who cried out, admitting his imperfect belief:

> "And Jesus said to him, 'If you can'! All things are possible for one who believes." Immediately the father of the child cried out and said, "I believe; help my unbelief!"
>
> Mark 9:23-24

Belief in someone or something only grows by testing it out. We ask, and we believe as much as our human mind can. God sees this faith and rewards this kind of testing out of our own ability to believe in spiritual happenings. We aren't Thomas, though, we have to believe without such a vivid personal touch.

I know God reaches us when we seek Him. He uses circumstances and other saints who help us. His timing is perfect. He seems to ignite all the senses, not only sight or touch but even taste and scent.

The same senses He created in us, He uses today to open our life up to receiving more and more spiritually. Think about the way a scent reminds you of a place or time. The taste of pumpkin spice takes most of us to Autumn. Our God-given senses have the ability to transport us, remind us, and move us in any given direction. We just have to stay alert, expecting God to engage with us, and when He does, believe Him as much as you humanly can.

I am blessed, although it has looked like I've been crushed. The blessing has been the way God has walked me through this divorce and the grief that it caused. I've learned things about myself I didn't know. I've experienced a love so unlike human love. Even the love within marriage or children is different from God's love, especially during a season of grief. It was God alone who showed me many difficult truths about others as well as myself.

He handed me truth. I reached out to receive it even though the pain felt hellish. He comforted me, and He lifted me out of one pit of mud and then another as I fell down again. Every pit was deeper and more dangerous.

I wondered. *What were his thoughts towards me, exactly? Did He grow tired of me?* What I felt was His mercy, patience, and loving kindness. His thoughts of me led to actions, His actions in all the unique ways He has of being present. I've shared many of them, but not all.

What a blessing it has been to know my God thinks of me. I flailed and fainted, despaired of life, yet He caught me. I lost my way a few times, yet He found me and nourished me back to health once again. I experienced how the life of Christ was so entangled vine-like, vise-like around my soul. He will never let me go.

I am not lost in a marriage tainted with deceit. He rescued me from that. I am not lost in a job I need for money, but it gives me absolutely no enjoyment. He told me to persevere and trust Him to provide, and I did. He reminded me that the ability to enjoy your work is a gift from Him and I boldly held my ground to live into that and not settle for anything less than God's best for me.

God has walked me through this time. He has not rescued my marriage or made everything concerning it any better at all. Actually, He seemed to light up the dark, shrouded places of the marriage and helped me realize the slow death it was causing both of us. There was no dramatic rescue but a quiet and gentle, slow walk. Where tears fell and hearts bled, anger erupted, and violence blinded my vision I was more than comforted.

For three years, we have walked together in this time frame called "after divorce." Vision for things I thought were never for me have been revived, and my soul is now full of hope. All the while, my ex and his new soon-to-be-wife were traveling to Italy and France and doing things I would have imagined were for my life at this stage.

But in reality, with my tender heart in the hands of my loving God, I could honestly admit that I never really wanted what they have or to do what they were doing. The world around me tried to convince me I had been cheated out of everything I had been work-ing towards in the marriage. As if I didn't get my reward, which I clearly deserved. I believed this, too, at times.

The truth is what I always dreamed of having was a career. A work of my own and the finances and independence that went with it. I longed for purpose and business endeavors. I desired to invest in things to make more out of it. This growth excited me. I would love to travel to the places they went and so many other places as well.

The beautiful thing is that I can travel and do exciting, fun things even alone (I might enjoy it more alone), but the deeper desire of my soul that I trust God put there is the normal everyday work that will welcome me back after these excursions. I won't stand there after all the fun is over and ask, "Now what?"

My day-to-day gets to be fun and exciting, but most importantly, my days are much more connected to my values. I'm not saying one way of life is better than another. What I am saying is this is my life, and what I know, for certain, is best for me. God chose it, not me or anyone else, and here I delight most in God because what He chose is actually perfect and beyond all I ever imagined my life could be.

It's as if God created me, knew me from the very beginning, loved me, and pursued me with his presence. His powerful presence is something that I cannot deny. His love draws me near, always reminding me who He is and who I am.

I want to choose life, and through Christ in me, I am learning how to keep myself alive. It's all so beautiful.

A Step Towards Life:

I hope you can think back on God's love and presence during your own divorce. How have you found his love differing from the love of other people? Is your belief in his love and ability to care for you growing stronger? It's been a journey, and wherever you are on the journey, know that you are not alone and you may make some mistakes or take a wrong turn, but God has a way of always finding us right where we are. You have a savior who invites you to believe his scars exist, and because of them, He can make your every scar a sacred place of healing.

www.ingramcontent.com/pod-product-compliance
Lightning Source LLC
Chambersburg PA
CBHW031417120626
46545CB00006B/2161